T0381097

CHRISTIAN LIVING STUDY GUIDE

Anthony L. Griffin, Kelser Weaver Jr,
Lavon Coles Jr

authorHOUSE®

AuthorHouse™
1663 Liberty Drive
Bloomington, IN 47403
www.authorhouse.com
Phone: 1-800-839-8640

First published by AuthorHouse 5/18/2009

ISBN: 978-1-4259-0017-5 (sc)

Printed in the United States of America
Bloomington, Indiana

This book is printed on acid-free paper.

Contents

Contents

Acknowledgments

I, **Anthony L Griffin**, first give thanks to my Lord and Savior Jesus Christ for the peace that surpasses all understanding He has given my wife and me after praying and seeking Him for direction in our lives and direction for our family. I was deployed to Iraq to work for one year or longer in support of Iraqi Freedom. I am very thankful to my wife and children, Kyle and my daughter Arielle, and her mother who helped support me in their prayers and shared the love of God while I was performing my military duties. I know the Lord has a purpose and plan for me in the Middle East. We knew God would get all the glory during this experience and testing time. I would also like to thank my pastor, Pastor Alonzo H. Pressley, and my home church, New Land New Seed Ministries of Augusta, Georgia, for all their prayers and support during this deployment to Iraq.

I would like to give a very special thanks to my wife, Mrs. Pamela H. Griffin, who has been my biggest supporter as a mother, wife, lover, and friend. She stands in the gap while I am deployed to Iraq. God has kept her strong in the faith, and she is the good thing the Lord has sent me. Thanks to my mother and father, Mr. John W. Griffin and Mrs. Annie L. Griffin, who live in Thomson, Georgia. My mother and father always told me to never quit or give up on anything. If I fail get back up and try again. My Dad reminded me that I am a Griffin. Just remember that fact and he would always support me if I needed anything. He said that we love you and care very much about you and your family. God has blessed my family, and I thank God every day for keeping them in His perfect will. I would also like to give thanks to the Christian House of Prayer family in Killeen, Texas, and a special thanks to one of my father's in the faith, pastor and bishop of the Christian House of Prayer, Bishop Nate Holcomb, a great man of God. He is a blessing to all the saints that are faithful in the House of Prayer. My faith went to another level during my tour in Texas. I would also like to give thanks to pastor and bishop of Zion Temple Church of God in Christ, Bishop Aledell Thomas, a great man of God. Thanks to the Church of God in Christ, Zion Temple family in Killeen. My time in the great state of Texas was very helpful in supporting me in growing more in the word of God. I am a better person because of all the good support systems that God has placed in my life to bring Him all the honor and glory. I say thanks be unto my Lord and Savior Jesus Christ who is doing a great work in my life. He does it all for His glory.

Out reach ministry of **New Land New Seed Ministries: Pastor Alonzo H. Pressley, Augusta, Georgia.**

Acknowledgments

    I, **Kesler Weaver, Jr.**, first give thanks to my Lord and Savior Jesus Christ for the peace that he gave me after finding out I would be deployed to Iraq for one year or longer in support of Iraqi Freedom. I am thankful to my wife and children who were willing to support me in my Military Carrier knowing the Lord had a purpose and plan for me during this experience. I give thanks to my parents for encouraging me in the Lord through the many difficult decisions that I was facing during this time. I am thankful to Bro. Sonny Scarbrough who begotten in the faith, my Church Family of "Simple House of Praise", and the many other Pastors and friends of the Mt. Vernon and Fairford Community for being understanding and willing to support me in the Lord through prayers and by sending care packages to me and my troops while in Iraq.

    The Lord has allowed me the time necessary and things needed for us to put this study together. The Lord first brought this idea to me through Bro. Anthony Griffin while deployed in support of Iraqi Freedom. This desert experience gave each of us the opportunity to come together in Brotherly Love and put these truths of God's Word into a study. Our goal is to pass on to you another tool that you can use to grow in your faith and be the Child of God that he has called you to be. May the Lord give you spiritual insight as to who you really are in Christ as you go through this new Christian study guide?

Your Brother in Christ
Kesler Weaver, Jr.
Presently Living in Malcomb, Alabama

Acknowledgments

I, **Lavon Coles, Jr**., first give thanks to my Lord and Savior Jesus Christ for His steadfast love for my family and me. I am extremely blessed and thankful God has always been a part of my life and has called me to this place of servitude. In the toughest days of my life, God has been faithful to deliver me. When the storm was calm, God has been there. He is the Great I Am. I give Him all the praise and glory for this opportunity to share the gospel of Jesus Christ. I give thanks to my wife for her continued support, for without her and God's grace and mercy, I would not be where I am today. She is an amazing woman who is the perfect fit for my life. Her remarkably wonderful commitment to God and our family has been the perfect complement to our life. For my mother, I am extremely thankful to have such a wonderful mother who cared enough for my salvation and ensured God's word was planted in my heart. To my wonderful mother-in law whom I love dearly and praise God, for she has been such an astounding inspiration in my life, and without her prayer and support, I might be lost today.

I am truly thankful for my children, who have been an absolute joy to my life. It was with their wonderful prayers that I was kept safe under God's wings during my deployment in Iraq. To the rest of my family, my sisters, brothers, and in-laws, for all their prayer, love, and support; I thank you all. I would also like to give thanks to Pastor James Hagan for guiding my growth in the word of God through his teachings and constant prayer for my family. Lastly, I would like to thank my brothers in Christ, Brother Griffin and Brother Weaver. It was their obedience to God and yielding to His Spirit that allowed God to minister to me and increase the love and presence of our Lord and Savior Jesus Christ in my life. Thank you, brothers, for this wonderful opportunity to share the gospel of Jesus Christ to a ding world. And the countless hours of teaching and sharing of your faith with me. Because of you, by the Grace of God, I stand ready for the wiles of the devil. God bless you all.

Put on the whole Armor of God that you may be able to stand against the wiles of the devil. For we do not wrestle against flesh and blood, but against principalities, against the powers and against the rulers of the darkness of this age, against spiritual hosts of wickedness in the heavenly places (Eph. 6:1 1-12).

May the Lord give you spiritual insight as to who you really are in Christ as you go through this study guide we have prepared.

Brother in Christ, **Lavon Coles, Jr.**

DO it and you will **BE** it, **KNOW** it then **SHOW** it, because you do **KNOW** it, if you show it.

KNOW THIS

DO THIS

BE THIS

POWERFUL

Griffin   Weaver   Coles

CHRISTIAN

LIVING

Study Guide

We used the Kingdom Keys mixed with our Faith.

Start using the correct Kingdom Keys, in God the Father the Son and the Holy Spirit. The Trinity three persons in one the Godhead and this is Doctrine concerning our faith and the (Greek word Dokein to seem; to appear to the observation or understanding).

Stop Living Backwards Today.

DO THIS AND BE CONVERTED AND KNOW THE POWER OF LIVING FOR GOD IN YOUR NEW CHRISTIAN LIFE.

LIVE FORWARD FROM THE EVIL, NEVER LIVING BACKWARD AGAIN.

THE DEVIL IS LIVING BACKWARDS.

DO NOT *GO BACK TO EVIL LIVING*

Book of Knowledge and Truth for *Powerful Christian Living*

DO NOT BE A CLOSET CHRISTIAN OR AN UNDERCOVER AGENT CHRISTIAN.

INTRODUCTION

Bible versions used and translations: KJV- (King James Version) NIV (New International Version) GNB- (Good News Bible) NLT-(New Living Translation), (Amplified Bible), (The Expositor Bible Counselor's Edition).

This study guide is for Christians to help us in our Christian walk so our lives will be changed all to the glory of God. God has saved us and we now have become children of the Most High God: We know He first loved us and gave us His Son so we could live with Him forever. While you are reading and studying this book, your mindset will be transformed for the better. You will start seeing yourself through the eyes of God, and begin to walk in the word like never before.

Take the time to get the knowledge that God can give. As you read, remember you are getting fresh oil and your cup is being filled. During this study, pray and ask God to help you, and trust that all will be done and you are doing what is pleasing to Him. Ask Him to give you a heart of flesh, so the words will bring Him all the glory.

You must die to self and live unto God and never look back again. We can clearly see the big picture by **FAITH** which stands for (forward action in the heavens). You must take a step forward by faith knowing that God is pleased by your faith plus your good works. Our lives will only change when we make the whole divine connection in the heavens and obey God's word while on the earth.

KNOWLEDGE OBJECTIVES AND GOALS

After the end of each lesson, you should be able to meet the objectives and goals.

1. Make some divine changes in your life and know God's word much better.

2. Explain and summarize the working of the Holy Spirit and the words the enemy uses to try and make negative changes in our walk with Christ.

3. Better define terms and words for us as Christians and know that we need to walk in discipleship and build our relationship as people of God with GOD.

4. See ourselves through the eyes of God and forget the world's way of seeing things and to stop living backwards and keep doing God's will.

5. Share more with our Christian brothers and sisters in group studies as we all grow in the spirit in the knowledge of Him who has called us.

6. Seek God more everyday and know the full power He has given to those who seek his righteousness and forget self (die to self) and live unto God.

7. Go to another level in Him (Christ) and be a disciple and a lover of God.

Book Dedication

To our family and, friends and all who will read this new Christian study guide of truth and knowledge of doing the will of our Lord and Savior, Jesus Christ, who has redeemed us from the hand of the enemy. We will only reach new levels of faith by obeying all of God's commandments and by fighting the good fight of faith which is in Christ Jesus our Lord.

We must be able to teach and instruct in the truth to all who hear and who wants to obey. Once we began to walk in the word having no shame, then we become true disciples of our Lord and Savior.

We ask you all in love to be true believers of the doctrine of Jesus Christ. We must stop playing church. Life is complete when we live the life we now have in Christ so study and pray and trust in God. He empowers us to walk in the Spirit and stop walking in the flesh with the devil. This book is written in truth to our family and friends, so that we may all live our life everlasting unto God.

We once walked in this darkness we now preach and teach about to all who listen; so harden not your hearts to the word of God, and we will eat the good of the land. Let us believe in God's holy word today. We shall live the good life which God can provide with much prayer and hope in Him. Once we begin to **do** our Father's will, we will be able to do all things in Him. We will be transformed by the washing of the word and given a new life to live in Christ.

Blessings and love, joy and peace have come upon us all through the new covenant our God has promised **us.** Please receive this by faith and in love. We have now been blessed of the Lord and highly favored forever. Remember God will not lie. Let us **do** this now and live looking forward to the future never looking back again at our pasts life. We must truly trust in God and lean not unto our own understanding, but in all our ways acknowledge Him and He will direct our paths. We have been truly blessed of the LORD.

Christians LIVE unto GOD
Looking Towards Our Future

The children of God will be our future, our tomorrow. The devil loves to see us do wrong and be sad with sorrows at a very early age. Satan is after us all because of the things that we have made our children learn about our GOD. We teach good values, morals, care and the love we need in Christ. We're always putting Him first, Jesus, our Lord. Where did we go wrong? How can this be? A child should not be holding a gun and staring at me with the look of darkness in his eyes, and a blank look on his face. Hanging out all night with his boys and terrorizing the place. Is this your child? Tell me it is not true, running the streets, and trying to be a gangster, selling his drugs and killing his own. No brotherly love. Where did we go wrong? Satan thought he had me, but a nation like ours is more powerful. We are big and proud and yes we say, "In God We Trust." We put it on our money and we say it with our lips. Is it in our hearts?

Our actions are different, are we hypocritical? The enemy inside of me is at war with the Spirit of GOD in me. We're good at fronting, lying, and cheating. I wonder if our future will be in danger, and we fall to defeat. What we need is to get back to God, fall on our faces, ask God for His forgiveness, and allow Him to show us how to be disciples. Pray together as a family and let our kids see us leading by example and showing love to one another as Jesus taught us. A change will come. With Christ in our life, we will receive the victory! We will teach our young men, and they will begin to put down their guns. We must teach them how to be fathers, and they must learn how to raise their own sons. We must be an example because we are lead by the manner in which Jesus Christ went to His Father. Tell your sons and daughters that **you** love them and tell them that Jesus Christ is the way, the truth and the life. We must show our love today and walk in it day by day. We do not have to fake it to make it in the kingdom of God. Obey God and not what man has to say. Remember God will provide all that we need in and through Christ Jesus our Lord and Savior. We must teach our young ladies how to be women of God, to treasure their bodies, and let God be in control of their bodies.

We must give our children the tools they need and teach them that they are to be mighty men and women of God. Now stand and see God move, knowing that you are great in God's eyes and you want to please God and make Him proud. We have been made whole and complete and we know what God wants for us now.

We know now that God is in control and without God we have no clear directions for our lives. Without God our dreams will die and our future is grim.

God wants us to seek His face and turn from our wicked ways and pray at all times. A nation will be destroyed because we did not trust in Him who has called us out of darkness. Let us get back to the basics and God will make a way out of no way. He will light the pathway in which we should walk and we will see it and our walk will be upright and pleasing in the sight of God. Let's start right now with **ME** and **YOU** now that we have GOD on our side! Help me lift up the name of Jesus to a dying world. Stand for Jesus Christ and his righteousness. Amen……

This Poem was written by the Griffin family: **Pamela Griffin** and my son **Kyle** and my daughter **Arielle.**

Blessed is a Nation whose God is the LORD of Lords and KING of Kings.

KNOW YOUR NUMBER ONE ENEMY

Do not go out looking for the enemy until you know who the enemy is that needs to be attacked. Let us study this enemy first. We will need to find out who is our number one enemy because the enemy who stands in the way of God's will, must be taken care of first and it must die. Christ can fill the empty place and start His good works as you begin to fight the good fight of faith with Him. The battle is not yours, it's the LORD's. So let me tell you who the number one enemy is. Yes, you are your number one enemy, which is the enemy in you that wants to walk with the flesh and do everything the way it wants to. Make no mistake about it, it's not your thing, and you cannot do what you want to or sock it to whoever you want to. You must obey God and die to yourself daily. Then we must know the power of submitting ourselves unto God and to resisting Beelz ebub, the chief of the evil spirits (the devil). **Titus 2: 11-12** for the grace of God that brings salvation has appeared to all men. Salvation is available to all on the basis of faith in Christ and what He did at the cross. 12 Teaching us that, denying ungodliness and worldly lusts tells us that it can be done. We should live soberly, righteously, and godly, in this present world. This can only be done by the Believer making the Cross the object of his or her faith which gives the Holy Spirit latitude to work in our lives bringing about the graces of God.

Titus 3:2 to speak evil of no man refers to the employment of the principle of grace, which excludes all violence of thoughts, languages, or actions, to be no brawlers, don't be contentious, but gentle as a fruit of the spirit [**Gal. 5:22-23**] gives us the fruits of the spirit, showing all meekness unto all men.

This portrays the inner grace of the soul, which can only be brought about in the life of the Believer by the Holy Spirit. He does these things strictly on the premise our faith in Christ and the finished work at the Cross. So with that being said here are some areas in which demon spirits work and move in the life of anyone that will let them operate in them. The first area is selfishness and wrongful use of pride, thinking it's about you, bitterness, jealousy, envy, lying, craftiness, deceitfulness, and lust. If any of these actions are working in you, they will tell you that you need to work harder on your development with the Holy Spirit to kill that enemy that is still at work in you. The enemy is trying to lead you away from the things of God and use you for his evil deeds. It makes you look like an undercover Christian and you will be an unproductive " aint", not a Saint of God.

But in Christ you can overcome the evil spirit that is within you, and you do not have to fake it to make it with Christ. God has said you do not have to act like you are obeying His word and walk by faith and in love because he knows us all. According to **James 1: 22** He commands us to be doers of His word and not just hearers only deceiving ourselves. Because God has already worked it all out and we are in the middle of the picture that is already painted. Now the truth is in your heart not in your head knowledge. God has set before you life or death and you must choose and remember the books are opened to the truth when it comes to you and God. See, once a picture is painted, it has captured all the words within the picture and only the author can tell you if his painting is finished or not. That's why Jesus

Christ is the author and finisher of our faith. The painter is the only one who will truly know all he sees in the picture that you are in, once it has been painted you must look to the painter (Christ).

This means you must seek out the painter to get some understanding and knowledge about you, once the painting has been done. The painter will tell you more and more once you get to know him in a personal way and you will get his insight about what he sees in you. The painter knows you and has a perfect photo of you on his file. **Roman 12:1-3** I beseech you therefore, brethren by the Mercies of God that you present your bodies a Living sacrifice holy, acceptable unto God which is your reasonable service **2** And be not conformed to this world but be ye transformed by the renewing of your mind, that you may prove what is that good and acceptable, and perfect, Will of God. **3** For I say, through the grace given unto me, to every man who is among you, not to think of himself more highly than he ought to think; but to think soberly, according as God has dealt to every man the measure of Faith this is given by the Holy Spirit at conversion. The definition of worldly is devoted to this world, and its pursuits, rather than spiritual affairs, so they are worldly wise possessing a practical and often shrewd understanding of human affairs which makes them worldly minded devoted to or engrossed in worldly interests.

Your name is in His book. You must stop being so worldly. You must just do all you can to find out how you look in His sight, and you must strive to keep that good look at all times. Now after all has been said and done you're a child of the King and your name has been changed to "whosoever." Your life is in Christ and the enemy that was in you is dead, and you now have the power of God at work in you, on you, and with you, in Jesus name.

Write your thoughts:

_____
_____
_____
_____

You must also know this Jesus is the author and finisher of your faith. And your faith must be tested so you will know that it is working for you. Whatever tries to come against you will not win, because you already got the victory in you. So call on the name of Jesus. Use the word to cast out any and all unrighteousness, and let faith go to work for you. Then the people will know that you know the true and living God and they cannot take you out of a painting of God, and you will not be blotted out of the picture by any person. Here is the revelation for you to put in your heart and live unto God. You are already in God's painting and he wants you to accept his Son so you can receive your sight to see the picture for yourself. Who you are is hidden in Christ with God's word, because it has been said a picture is worth a thousand words, which is a true statement, for all to say. Jesus is the author and finisher of our faith for a life in Him.

Stop being disobedient, learn self control, and **do** the things God has commanded you to **do.** Have self control and your faith will increase in the book of Romans the word is very clear to all willing hearts that will hear and obey God's word. **Romans 6:-16-17: Do** you not know that to whom you present yourselves slaves to obey, you are that one's slaves whom you obey, whether of sin leading to death, or obedience leading to righteousness? 17 But God be thanked that though you were slaves of sin, yet you **obeyed** from the heart that form of doctrine to which you were delivered. So just **do** it (be obedient and head down the path to righteousness) and you will truly **be** "it "for the greater one is the only one in you working on your "can do." The word says according to **Philippians 4:13** I can do all things through Christ that strengthens me. You must know this to walk in victory. That's what you **do** every time the enemy tries to stand up against your life. The devil's d-words in this book are just some of the words, he will try to use on us. You need to know **them** and keep **them** out of your mouths and **do** not let them in your heart. The devil knows who you belong to, and God knows whom you will obey so choose you this day whom you will obey (God or Satan).

Just remember the life you choose you will live, so choose to **do God's word** and not **be** fooled by your head knowledge. Head knowledge is needed in common everyday life and helps to advance in the world's eye. But in the now, it takes faith and trust in the kingdom of God. You must use your heart and trust your heart, because God sees and knows your heart. In **Proverbs 4:23** it says, Keep thy heart with all diligence; for out of it are the issues of life. So feed your heart God's word and it will grow strong. You must **know** and get the words of God deeply planted in your heart and start to walk in what you receive and believe it. Because you are what you believe. **Do** not reject the power of God's truth. Get an, understanding which God freely gives to those who ask Him. Change your life.

NOTES: _____
_____
_____
_____
_____
_____
_____
_____
_____
_____
_____
_____
_____
_____
_____

Remember this key factor while you are studying this study guide:

Your flesh does not want to hear this but the Bible tells us that your spirit man is willing and the flesh is weak. So fill up your spirit with some high spiritual fuel so that it will help your heart run better and faster and smoother while you run this race with Christ. Here are some key words to think about during your reading and studying about your number one enemy. Ask yourself am I jealous? Am I hiding my iniquity from others? Am I a self-righteous and a stiff necked person? Am I a rebel? Is my mouth corrupted with bad words? If so, your fruit is of the devil and not for anyone who calls on the name of the LORD.

Read and study: Job 31:25-34, Jeremiah 6:15-16, Deuteronomy 32:16, Psalms 79:5, Deuteronomy 4:24, Romans 13:13, Proverbs 19:25, Proverbs 10:12, Philippians 1:15-16

When you look in the word at all times and follow the word of God notice the words **"Do" and "Now"** in bold letters. Notice "**now,**" "**do,**" "be,", "us" and "them."

You must remember to hide these meaningful words you in your heart. It is never about you; but it is all about Him and He is using us to bring Him glory. It is safe to say that it is "us" (believers) against "them" (unbelievers). We have the victory over them once we know and do what our heavenly Father has commanded (told) us to **do.** We will be whatever we do, all things to the glory of God. A true child of God will produce the good fruits and be deeply rooted and grounded in Christ, always doing things pleasing to God our Father.

Read and study: (**Hebrews 6: 1-10**) to get the foundation of the gospel. Know the fruit you are <u>producing</u> and work hard to keep the weeds out of the garden of your life. You now live unto God. Read and study (the fruit of God's spirit **Galatians 5:22-26**). You must produce God's fruit:

Write notes:

_____
_____
_____
_____
_____
_____
_____
_____
_____
_____
_____
_____
_____
_____

The people of God must keep planting if you are already planting God's word in you. Again I say to you look at all of the following words in bold letters. Know "**now**", "**do,**" "**be,**" "**us,**" "**them**". You must remember to hide these meaningful words in your heart. Know that it is never about you, but it is all about Him and He is using us to bring Him glory. So it is safe to say that it is us against them. We have the victory over them once we know and do according to the word. If you are not planting the word of God, start doing it today. The word must be planted every day. Then you start looking for a good harvest in due season if you faint not. I know that you know He has redeemed you from the hand of the devil. Just

do it and you will be it and people will see it and **know** you have over-come your number one enemy and now you're ready to help win the big battle.

Let us <u>fight</u> the good fight of faith, because without faith it is impossible to please God (**Hebrews11:6**) Keep on fighting the good fight of faith. We got the devil beat hands down. The book of **Hebrews 11:1** tells us in the first two words in the text it won, because, "**now** faith" is those two words you must mix word with faith now. We just need to look to the LORD and know that faith is with God and reading his word feeds the spirit to help your faith and never going backwards and seeing your faith has **won** the victory, when "**now**" is when you want your faith to work. Study that chapter and ask God to reveal more of the text to you during your studies of the book of Hebrews, starting with chapter 11. Let your faith go to work more in your life and you will see <u>God's</u> hand moving mightily in your life. The question is when, and the answer is **Now**…. Amen

Luke 9:2

Then He sent them to proclaim the Kingdom of God and to heal the sick.

Luke 9:23

And He said to them all, If any man will come after Me, let him deny himself, and take up his cross daily and follow Me.

Take up your cross daily and follow Jesus.
Luke 9:2   Men in the Army of the Lord

Griffin, Anthony L.

Cole, Jr. Lavon

Weaver, Jr. Kesler

Kingdom Keys

It is not about you, but it is all about Jesus.

It's ALL COVERED under the BLOOD so you do not have to fake it to make it.

SHOW THEM YOU KNOW THEM

The bible is very clear to the Christians who walk in the light and the glory of God. Ecclesiastes means "called out ones literally, preacher" and Ecclesiastes 5:1 says, "Keep thy foot when thou goest to the house of God, and be more ready to hear, than to give the sacrifice of fools: for they consider not that they do evil."

Ecclesiastes 8:12-13: though a sinner do evil an hundred times, and his days be prolonged, yet surely I know that it shall be well with them that fear God, which fear before him: But it shall not be well with the wicked, neither shall he prolong his days, which are as a shadow; " because he feareth not before God."

Ecclesiastes 12:1: Remember now thy Creator in the days of thy youth, while the evil days come not, nor the years draw nigh, when thou shalt say I have no pleasure in them;

Chapter 12 of Ecclesiastes has much to say to us about them if we walk in the word of God. It will show them because He wants us to stand out and be wise and fear Him and have a teachable spirit and to do good at all times and overcome evil.

Read and study chapter 12 of Ecclesiastes and write notes as you study the message from the text. The word knowledge will show you them because when God is speaking about knowledge, He is talking about heart knowledge not head knowledge.

Note: _____
_____
_____
_____
_____
_____
_____
_____

Colossians 2:1-7 gives us a good message to them from us and it comes from a word of knowledge. We must show them that He is at work in us. 1 For I would that ye knew what great conflict I have for you, and for them at Laodicea, and for as many as have not seen my face in the flesh; 2 That their hearts might be comforted, being knit together in love, and unto all riches of the full assurance of understanding to the acknowledgement of the mystery of God, and of the Father, and of Christ; 3 **In whom are hidden all the treasures of wisdom and knowledge.** 4 And this I say, points directly to the false teachers, lest any man should beguile you with enticing words refers to being deceived by subtle reasoning. 5 For though I be absent in the flesh, yet am I with you in the spirit, joying and beholding your order, and the steadfastness of your Faith in Christ. 6 As ye have therefore received Christ Jesus the Lord, so walk ye in Him: 7 Rooted and built up in Him pertains to a proper foundation, and stablished in the faith, in Christ and the Cross, as you have been taught refers to the Colossians coming in the right way, but some of them considering the false message of the Gnostics.

The word Gnostics comes from the Latin word gnosticus, and from greek word gnstikos which is of **knowledge.** Now once you begin to walk in Him you will be showing them you **know** Him and walk in the **knowledge** of Him who has called you out of darkness into His light for life in Christ Jesus.

1 John 2:1-6
My little children, these things I write to you, so that you may not sin. And if anyone sins, we have an Advocate with the Father, Jesus Christ the righteous. 2 And He Himself is the propitiation for our sins, and not for ours only but also for the whole world. 3 Now by this we know that we know Him, if we keep His commandments. 4 He who says, "I know Him" and does not keep His commandments, is a liar and the truth is not in him. 5 But whoever keeps His word, truly the love of God is perfected in him. By this we know that we are in Him. 6 He who says he abides in Him ought himself also to walk just as He walked.

Also with this word Gnostics we get Gnosticism which is a system of false teachings that existed during the early centuries of Christianity. Where they believed that knowledge was the way to salvation, which we know as New Testament believers that Jesus is the only way and the knowledge in Him we do and trust in the finished work at the Cross.

Now let us study a few important words. Through etymology we can see, and understand that the usage of words and how they change in times past can relay a different message by tracing its transmission from one language to another. So the key is that you **must be developed in your knowledge of Him.** We must use God word and your thinking and purpose must be set on God's kingdom, and be pleasing Him. Put your hope and trust in God and not in man or trying to please man , then God will give you favor with man in whom He made.

Romans 8:28 states that we **know** that all things work together for the good to them who love God, to them who are the called according to His purpose. **So in order to go to a new level in Christ Jesus you must be developed in your mind, to the things of God and know all the glory is unto God and we thank God for using us to do His perfect will.**

1. **Knowledge** is a two part word with a hidden word in it. The first word being "know" and the second part being "ledge" and another hidden word is **now** in knowledge. The definition of knowledge is the fact of knowing what is truly known. As believers and the body of truth, our knowledge comes from the Holy one and is spiritual discerned by our spirit from God and not just information, and principles acquired by humankind.

2. God tells us to get knowledge is the understanding of the truth of His word, and to fear Him once you get it your knowledge from the spirit will be greater than man's. 2 Peter 1: 3 and 5- 6 says it like this: According as his divine power hath given unto

us all things that pertain unto life and godliness, through the knowledge of him that called us to glory and virtue:

5 And beside this, giving all diligence, add to your faith virtue; and to virtue knowledge;

6 And to knowledge temperance; and to temperance patience; and patience godliness. We need life and godliness through the knowledge of him who called us by his own glory and goodness." Remember this statement about knowledge. The Holman Christian Standard Bible makes it very plane and clear in Proverbs 8: 7-9 for my mouth tells the truth, and wickedness is detestable to my lips. 8. All the words of mouth are righteous; none of them are deceptive or perverse. 9. All of them are clear to the perceptive, and right to those who discover knowledge.

Seek God and ask God for understanding and growth in the knowledge of His Son and walk in His divine power. Then start to live upright before them and show them you know Him who has all power.

3. The bible helps us and it gives us the commands from God and the instructions we must follow and know. Hosea 4:6 says "My people are destroyed for a lack of knowledge: because thou hast rejected knowledge, I will also reject thee, that thou shalt be no priest to me: seeing thou hast forgotten the law of thy God, I will also forget thy children."

Write notes on what the Holy Spirit has spoken to your heart and what you have gained already up to this point of the lesson.

_____

_____

_____

_____

_____

_____

_____

1 John 2:1-6 My little children, these things I write to you, so that you may not sin. And if anyone sins, we have an Advocate with the Father, Jesus Christ the righteous. 2 And He Himself is the propitiation for our sins, and not for ours only but also for the whole world. 3 Now by this we know that we know Him, if we keep His commandments. 4 He who says, "I know Him," and does not keep His commandments, is a liar, and the truth is not in him. 5 But whosoever keeps His word, truly the love of god is perfected in him. By this we know that we are in Him. 6 He who says he abides in him ought himself also to walk just as He walked.

We should do what we have been commanded to do and learn to obey the word of God and stop giving into the flesh and walking like them which is the old man's way. We are new creatures in Christ and they can see you know Him, because of your daily walk is to follow the spirit of the living God.

Colossians 3:16: Let the word of Christ dwell in you richly in all wisdom; teaching and admonishing one another in psalms and hymns and spiritual songs, singing with grace in your hearts to the Lord.

Now with the word in you and you obeying the inner man and walking in the spirit of truth, they will know who your Father is and whom you serve without you telling them anything. God's love will do all things for you and no one can stop it from happening.

They can only see the effects of God's goodness, grace and mercy at work in you and on your life. Jesus went to the Father on our behalf so that we can be children of God and become sons and daughters of God, as we mature spiritually. Then the whole world will know about us as we walk in the full assurance of faith in the kingdom of God, all for his glory and telling His story.

This is what Jesus said in **John 17:11-19, 21-23:**

"And now I am no more in the world, but these are in the world, and I come to thee. Holy Father, keep through thine own name those whom thou hast give me, that they may be one, as we are.

12 While I was with them in the world, I kept them in thy name: those that thou gavest me I have kept, and none of them is lost, but the son of perdition; that the scripture might be fulfilled.13 And now come I to thee; and these things I speak in the world, that they might have my joy fulfilled in themselves.

14 I have given them thy word; and the world hath hated them, because they are not of the world, even as I am not of the world. 15 I pray not that thou shouldest take them out of the world, but that thou shouldest keep them from the evil.

16 They are not of the world, even as I am not of the world. 17 Sanctify them through thy truth: thy word is truth. 18 As thou hast sent me into the world, even so have I also sent them into the world.19 And for their sakes I sanctify myself, that they also might be sanctified through the truth.

21"That they all may be one; as thou, father, art in me, and tin thee that they also may be one in us: that the world may believe that thou hast sent me.

23 I in them, and thou in me, that they may be made perfect in one; and that the world may know that thou hast sent me, and hast loved them, as thou hast loved me.

We must be people of truth with a calling on our life. We must be a community of believers full of the Holy Ghost which, works in us because we were once like them until we came into the saving knowledge of Christ through the word of God.

We are the New Testament Church which started in the book of Acts so let's see what Acts has to say to us **Acts 2:47:** "Praising God, and having favor with all the people and the Lord added to the church daily such as should be saved.

Please read **Acts 23: 9-47** and pray and study the importance of fellowship with the body once you know you have been redeemed. We must show it once we get it, and they will know we got it all to the glory of God. There is a blessing in truly knowing who Jesus Christ is. Amen…

YOU CANNOT GO TO HELL? (IF)

This is a statement that sometimes thought to be true. Many people don't even believe in hell. They think that there is only a heaven. When we research the scriptures, we see that Jesus spoke on hell more than he spoke about heaven. Once a person comes to truly know Jesus as Lord and, Savior, they know this type of thinking is a mistake. Many people say that surely the God of goodness and mercy would not send anyone to hell.

In fact that is true. He doesn't actually send anyone to hell, but people who reject God's love and mercy (which is in Jesus) send themselves to this awful place that God didn't make for man. We know the bible teaches us that God is love. By His great love He made away that we could be reconciled (forgiven from sin and restored) back unto Himself and assured of everlasting life. All of His love was wrapped up in his beloved son Jesus Christ. Let's examine this love that God has for man.

1 John 4:7-11 says 7"Beloved, let us love one another: for love is of God; and every one that loveth is born of God and knoweth God. 8. He that loveth not, knoweth not God; for God is love." 9. In this was manifested the love of God toward us, because God sent his only begotten son into the world, that we might live through Him. 10. Here in is love, not that we loved God, but that He loved us, and sent his Son to be the propitiation for our sins. 11. Beloved, if God so loved us, we ought also to love one another." As we see in 1John God's love toward us is far more gracious than we can ever imagine. We are all sinners because of the falling away of Adam. We see that God's love toward us was so great that he gave his own son to be crucified for our sins. One of the most; quoted scriptures in the bible is John 3:16 which states "For God so loved the world that he gave his only begotten son that whosoever believeth in him shall not perish but have everlasting ,life." Jesus gives us insight into the depth of God's love for man. Jesus was sent down from heaven for the primary purpose of being the mediator and the burden bearer and to set the example for us to live by as Christians. The example we should follow is the ensample of Christ wherein we take a sample of Christ and let in work in us.

Notes:
_____
_____
_____
_____
_____
_____
_____

We see here in 1 John how he begins by telling the church in this letter to love each other. This love he is speaking about is God's love, not the conditional love we know from the carnal side of man. But the word of God is without condition to all who will obey it and get in position to receive from the LORD. He states here also, he that shows or demonstrates this kind of love is born of God. Well, you say, it is hard to share your love with some people, especially those who won't let you love them. God said to do it with His love which he gives to us unconditionally even when they continue to say and do things that make it hard for anyone to love them. As Christians we still have to let the love of God in us be extended without thinking about what they do or say to us.

In John chapter one, we see this love manifested in Jesus Christ. John states that he was not that Light, but was sent to bear witness of that Light. John 1: 9"The true Light, which lighteth every man that cometh into the world." He accepted the Father's will to come down to this earth and become the payment for our sins so, that we could have eternal life through Him. This is the key that unlocks the door and sets our soul free from destruction and hell. Once we have truly repented of our sins and accepted Jesus as our Lord and Savior, we are children of the Light. Hell is not an option anymore. So give praise unto the LORD. We won't go to hell, because our sins have been forgiven. Now we must walk in repentance and confess our sins and obey the word in 1 John 1:9 "If we confess our sins he is faithful and just to forgive us our sins, and to cleanse us from all unrighteousness." That is God's desire for us in Christ Jesus.

Let's take a look at some scriptures that will point us toward God's desire for mankind.

1. **Luke 13:5** "I tell you, Nay; but, except ye repent, ye all likewise perish."
   Comment: Repentance allows us to be honest before God and to seek forgiveness for any sin we have committed,

Notes or your own personal comment: _____
_____
_____
_____
_____

2. **1 John 1:9**, "If we confess our sins, he is faithful and just to forgive our sins, and cleanse us from all unrighteousness."
   Comment: Through our confessions we acknowledge sin and receive forgiveness for what was done and it is put under the blood of Jesus for complete forgiveness

3. **John 14:6** "Jesus said unto him, I am the way, the truth, and the life: no man cometh to the Father, but by me." Comment: We see that the father has committed all things to the Son and eternal life only comes through Jesus Christ.

4. **2 Timothy 1:9-10** "Who hath saved us, and called us with a holy calling, not according to our works, but according to his own purpose and grace, which was given us in Christ

Jesus before the world began; But is now made manifest by the appearing of our Savior Jesus Christ, who hath abolished death, and hath brought life and immortality to light through the gospel."Comment: Jesus came to bring us the eternal life that God desired for us to have from the beginning of the world. Through his death, burial, and resurrection: we were given the opportunity to be restored to a right relationship with God.

Notes or personal comments:

_____

_____

_____

_____

_____

_____

5. **Ephesians 2:8-10** "For by grace are ye saved through faith; and that not of yourselves: it is the gift of God: 9 Not of works, lest any man should boast. 10. For we are his workmanship, created in Christ Jesus unto good works, which God hath before ordained that we should walk in them."

Let's go back to this misconception that hell is a myth and that people really don't go to hell. We see throughout the bible that the scripture tells us that God's desire for us is not to go to hell. We also see through His word that hell is in fact a real place. Let's take a moment and examine what Jesus said: Luke 16:19-31says "There was a certain rich man, which was clothed in purple and fine linen, and fared sumptuously every day: 20 And there was a certain beggar named Lazarus, which was laid at his gate, full of sores, 21 And desiring to be fed with the crumbs which fell from the rich man's table: moreover the dogs came and licked his sores. 22 And it came to pass, that the beggar died, and was carried by the angels into Abraham's bosom: the rich man also died, and was buried; 23And in hell he lifted up his eyes, being in torments, and seeth Abraham afar off, and Lazarus in his bosom.24 And he cried and said, Father Abraham, have mercy on me, and send Lazarus that he may dip the tip of his finger in water, and cool my tongue; for I am tormented in this flame.

Comment: We know that despite what the devil might tell us or do to us our salvation is by faith in Jesus Christ. We could never be just good enough to earn it but by good works and by the grace of God by faith we are saved. Christianity is a living faith because Jesus is a living Savior ruling and reigning in our hearts for life.

25 But Abraham said, Son, remember that thou in thy lifetime receivedst thy good things, and likewise Lazarus evil things: but now he is comforted, and thou art tormented. 26 And beside all this, between us and you there is a great gulf fixed: so that they which would pass from hence to you cannot; neither can they pass to us that would come from thence.
27 Then he said, I pray thee therefore, father, that thou wouldest send him to my father's house: 28 For I have five brethren; that he may testify unto them, lest they also come into this place of torment. 29 Abraham saith unto him, they have Moses and the prophets; let them

hear them.30 And he said, Nay, father Abraham: but if one went unto them from the dead, they will repent. 31 and he said unto him, if they hear not Moses and the prophets, neither will they be persuaded, though one rose from the dead.

Luke *12:4-5* "And I say unto you my friends, be not afraid of them that kill the body, and after that have no more that they can do. 5 But I will forewarn you whom ye shall fear: Fear him, which after he hath killed hath power to cast into hell; yea, I say unto you, Fear him."

Comment: We see here in this passage of scripture that Jesus was talking about a literal place and a real person who went there and did not like it. Stop and just try to visualize this illustration in your mind of the horrible place called hell. We all suffer through many things in life, but it is still hard to imagine a place this horrific. So you can see there was no comforting this rich man, and he was not able to leave this place. Hell is no joke. It's a place we should not want anyone to find themselves in. It is so important that we as Christians be about our Father's business, telling the world of God's saving grace.

Notes: _____
_____
_____
_____
_____

We see the reality of this place called hell as we study God's word and as he reveals His divine truths by the Holy Spirit. There has been something instilled into the hearts of people around the world today called fear. But it's the world's type of fear, not the fear of the LORD. With all the terrorist acts, killings, immorality, disease, unstable weather conditions, and the list goes on and on. Many people in the world today are looking for safety and security.

All of mankind has the desire to feel secure and safe from danger. The devil, Satan, is doing everything in his power to crush man and entangle him with the sins that separate him from God. He puts fear in the hearts of man and tries to focus man's attention on the problems by leaving out the answer **(Jesus is the answer).**

Notes: _____

We must that Jesus Christ has come to Save us and make us free forever with Him.
_____
_____
_____
_____
_____

We must place our trust in Jesus Christ, and we have nothing to fear but God. The fear of God is out of reverence to His divine power. No matter what man says or does to **us,** we have peace and security in Christ. Despite what comes or what goes, we must hold fast to the word of God, in faith. We shouldn't let our hearts be burdened down with the troubles in this life. Remember what the psalmist said in Psalms 27:1" The LORD is my light and my salvation; whom shall I fear?

The LORD is the strength of my life; of whom shall I be afraid? "

So read and study these scriptures and ask God give you revelation knowledge of His word and help you in your Christian walk daily as pick up your cross and follow Him.

1. **Job 11:18-19**
2. **Deuteronomy33:12**
3. **Proverbs18:10**
4. **Isaiah 43:1-2**
5. **Psalms 4:8**
6. **Matthew 11:28**
7. **John 16:33**

Remember you cannot go to hell once you have repented of your sins and accepted Jesus Christ. Once you have completed this study you will truly know what do you about every being afraid of going to hell.

Have you ever heard the saying that knowledge is power? Now you know that the knowledge we need is in the Holy one Jesus Christ. "And just knowing is half the battle?" God tells us that the battle is not our but the Lords and we must stay in the fight and fight the good fight of faith. So you see I have heard these sayings many times in my life, but never really took time to analyze them with truth. There is a spiritual link to these phrases, that is a spiritual understanding of the decisive meaning imbedded within these phrases. I want to take time to share with you the other half of the battle and the power exhibited behind knowing.

Ask yourself the question what do you know about God? Take a few minutes to reflect on what you know about God. If someone were to ask you to describe what God is like, could you? What does He look like? Does He have a sense of humor? Does God get angry? How big is He? If you have children someday they might ask you some of these very questions. Even if you don't have children be prepared for one of your friends to ask you what God is like, because when they enter the family of God, they become childlike in Christ. They become inquisitive and thirst for the Lord. As Christians, we must stand ready for that one person who God puts in our path for us to minister to.

The Bible tells us in 2 Timothy 2:15:"Study to show thyself approved unto God a workman that needeth not be ashamed rightly dividing the word of truth be diligent to present yourself approved to God." This is our direction to study God's word. Now in studying God's word, we will rightly attain a level of knowledge to prepare us for our walk with Christ. Along with this will be various opportunities where you will be the only Bible someone may ever read. You may be the only way of escape for the lost person who is desperately seeking God.

Can you think of someone in your family who desperately needs to come to know the Lord? I can. My desire is to joyously celebrate the second coming of Christ with all, but I know what God has revealed to me through His word. That is that not everyone will receive Him. Many will reject Him. This tells us there will be some that go to hell. Make sure that you are not one of them.

Jesus made this point very clear in Matthew 7:13-14 which states "Enter by the narrow gate; for wide is the gate and broad is the way that leads to destruction, and there are many who go in by it. Because narrow is the gate and difficult is the way which leads to life: and there are few who find it." Jesus tells us it will be difficult. I don't know about you, but I have encountered many difficult tasks during my life. With those difficult moments in front of me, I needed a certain measure of knowledge to succeed. Unless I possessed the level of knowledge necessary, I would have never been able to complete the harder tasks. We can apply a similar analogy to our walk through life. The Bible teaches us that we will experience trials and tribulations.

Even as Christians, we will endure many afflictions. But do you know that God has given us a way out of whatever temptation comes our way. First know that temptation is not of God, but of Satan who is known as the temper. Read James 1:12-13 God allows testing for the purpose of strengthening our faith and character, while Satan entices us with evil for the purpose of destruction. In every test, God provides a way of escape. The word of God tell us that no temptation has overtaken you except such as is common to man; but God is faithful, who will not allow you to be tempted beyond what you are able, but with the temptation will also make the way of escape, that you may be able to bear it.

2 Peter 2:20 "For if after they have escaped the pollutions of the world through the **knowledge** of the Lord and Savior Jesus Christ, they are again entangled therein, and overcome, the latter end is worse with them than the beginning."

Study in a study group and pray with each other and see the power of God's holy word begin to work mightily in the life of everyone who obeys God word.

God commands us to be faithful until death and great is your reward.

DEVIL'S D-WORD

Let us learn the devil's d-words and cast **them** out of our vocabulary. Tell the devil that he can go to hell by himself, and that you are going to start living for God.

You must be developed in your thinking (**mind**) in order to walk in the deliverance that comes from the word of God that believers of God must understand and speak. It is never for **them (the non-Christians)** because the devil comes to you to find out what you know about them and to see if you know God's word. This is not what most Christians want to hear because of what they do every day which includes failing to read and study God's word. The Bible is not a feel good book, so remember you are what you believe.

The Bible will help us to live as powerful Christians. Luke declares to us in the book of **Luke 1:1- 4, 1** "For as much as many have taken in hand to set forth in order a declaration of those things which are most surely believed among us. **2** Even as they delivered them unto us, which from the beginning were eyewitnesses, and ministers of the Word. **3** It seemed good to me also having had perfect understanding of all things from the very first, means that he made absolutely certain of the reliability of these " eyewitness accounts" to write unto you in order, refers to and orderly design, not necessarily in chronological order, most excellent Theophilus."

Now the definition of **Theophilus** is a lover of God and there are some things that the people of God must **KNOW** if they truly love God**.** There must be some proof of your love for God, your love must be proven after your confession because your **confession is your possession** that you love the LORD. **4** "That you might know the certainty of those things wherein you have been instructed."

The definition of possession is the act of having or taking into control. Control or occupancy of property without regard to ownership, something owned, occupied, or controlled. Possession is also a psychological state in which an individual's normal personality is replaced by another to have as an attribute, knowledge, or skill. We must be possessed by Christ because Christ develops us from within and the Lord will direct us to the end. In Jesus' name we are delivered and set free.

As you get to know the devil's plots, you will notice that he will always use what you see to combat your faith. As a God seeker, we walk by faith and not by sight, and we must always be ready to give an answer for the hope that lies within us and we must always stand on God's word.

II Corinthians 4:8-9 verse **8** states "Let us know that we are troubled on every side, yet not **distressed**; we are perplexed, but not in despair **9** Persecuted, but not forsaken cast down, but not destroyed." Make no mistake the devil is mad about the truth being revealed in this book. God has given us the power to speak up and use His word to speak to all who will hear. Obey these words of truth and they will improve your walk with Him once you learn to **do** His will. God revealed me to myself and began a work in me to get my life in order. My flesh was in control until Christ took over, and the anointing was poured out on my life by the Anointed One.

Always have a pen and paper when you set down to read and study God's word, and write what God has revealed to you. Our life is an open book. We must reveal our life to others, so the next generation will not fall into the same sins that once held us. Peter <u>said</u> "When thou are converted strengthen thy brother." This is a commandment from God. We must **do** the same as Peter. We know that we have overcome the devil with the word of truth and the power of the Holy Spirit operating in us, all to the glory of God, for life in Christ Jesus. Once we know we have been converted unto God, we must do what God commands.

We can combat them (devil D-words) better if we know what they really mean and we realize that they kill our faith. God wants us to speak His word and mix it with faith and be over comers and keep all unclean words out of our mouths.

Conduct a word study and share your findings with a group on the revelation that was imparted, to you during your word study. Define the words in biblical terms and notice that you may have different definitions of the words.

1. *You must have a scripture to counteract the devils D-word because only God's word will give you victory over the devils D-words.*
2. *You will have different scriptures to combat Satan's D-words but you must be able to explain your findings to the group.*

The devil's d- words are words that the devil uses and wants us to believe but God will reveal the true meaning of them to you in His word. This is just a few of the many words that Satan attempts to use against the body of Christ.

1. *Disobey:* _____
   _____
   _____
   _____
   _____

2. *Disconnected:* _____
   _____
   _____
   _____
   _____

3. *Discouraged:* _____
   _____
   _____

4. Divorce: _____
_____
_____

5. Devilish: _____
_____

6. Disapproved: _____
_____
_____

7. Division: _____
_____
_____
_____

8. Disturb: _____
_____
_____
_____
_____

9. Disloyal: _____
_____
_____
_____

10. Deprived: _____
_____
_____
_____

11. *Disgrace:* _____
_____
_____
_____
_____

12. *Discomfort:* _____
_____
_____
_____
_____

13. *Depressed:* _____
_____
_____
_____
_____

14. *Disfigured:* _____
_____
_____
_____
_____

15. *Discriminate:* _____
_____
_____
_____
_____

16. *Discredit:* _____
_____
_____
_____
_____

17. *Demons:* _____
_____
_____
_____

18. *Dummy:* _____
_____
_____

_____
_____

19. *Disowned:* _____
_____
_____
_____

20. *Disorganized:* _____
_____
_____
_____

21. *Denounce:* _____
_____
_____
_____

22. *Debauchery:* _____
_____
_____
_____

23. *Distract:* _____
_____
_____
_____

24. *Discussed:* _____
_____
_____
_____

25. *Destroyed:* _____
_____
_____
_____

26. Death: _____
_____
_____
_____

27. Divide: _____
_____
_____
_____

28. Doomed: _____
_____
_____
_____
_____

There are many more words that start with "d" that we can add to this list, but they have no controlling thoughts that keep you in bondage as most of these words do. So as Christians we must study God's word and look up words that stand out in our spirit and have great impact on us as Believers. So let's study them and keep the d-words out of our heart and out of our mouth so that we will not give the devil a foot hold and he cannot get a stronghold on us. Let's not give place to the devil ever again. **God is our Strong Hold for life in Christ.**

1. Know the **devil, Satan, the number one adversary of God and Christ.**
    He is the king of all evil deeds and the master and father of sin. He controls all mischievous behavior. He is better known as the wicked one and the master of lies.

2. Know his **demons**, an evil spirits that poses people.
    The devil controls the demons and they carry out his orders and commands and seek whom they may devour;

3. Watch what you are **doing.**

4. Know how to identify **d- fool"** who is silly or senseless person. He is right in his own eyes. One who is deficient in judgment, sense, or understanding. One that can be easily tricked or dupe. The "d-fool" has said in his heart there is no God.

5. Know how to identify **"d- player"** who is a person who takes advantage of **others'** feelings. And "d-player" is a **pretender** or a **cool <u>fool</u> who** has not been found out. They always emphasize or publicize their dirty works. They can be undercover lovers with more than one lover. They behave irresponsibly or deceitfully. They can be male or female. Let the truth be told the best player is a "**d**ead player" They must give up d-player life and turn to the truth and live again.

6. Know how to identify **d-liars**; one who makes false statements deliberately presented as true. They know how to convey a false image or impression of the truth, better known as twisted truths or half-truths. **Note that a liar loves when a lie has been told because a lie does not care who tells it, it just wants to be told.**

Powerful Christians must know that what, ever you **do** will determine what you will **be** and your **do** will never exceed your **be.**

So learn this teaching and **do** what you have been instructed to **do** by God. If you say you're a child of God then stop doing the things the old flesh man enjoyed. Live in the new life you have chosen with the power of God's Spirit. A person is alienated from life with God because of the ignorance that is in them known as "(self)". You are the only one blocking your blessings and delaying the power of the Holy Spirit to work in you.

Notes:

_____
_____
_____
_____
_____
_____
_____
_____
_____

Let us **do** the work of the One who has called us out of darkness into His marvelous light. Christ is our redeemer and we know we have been redeemed from Satan. The devil tempts us, and if we obey he will keep us from our destiny.

It is very important for us to **do** the right things and stop obeying Satan. We must walk in the spirit of Christ because we are doer of God's will.

God commands us in the book of Romans to **be** not conformed to this world or this age. Do not be fashioned after it and adapted to the world's external, superficial customs.

We must be renewed in our minds so that we may prove what is that good and acceptable and perfect will of God, is for your life. (Romans 12:2)

We now have the power to **do** this because the book of Ephesians said He dwells in our hearts by faith. It is by faith we can please God and **do** His will in love and truth. Be children of the light. We now know of and have given our lives to the truth and teachings of Christ Jesus, our Lord and Savior. Let us not continue in sin any longer if we call on the name of Jesus. We are not walking in darkness anymore because the light has come into our hearts. Ephesians 2:2 Wherein time past ye walked according to the course of this world, according to the prince of the power of the air, the spirit that now worketh in the children of disobedience. Your body is flesh, but walking in the flesh means, that you are fulfilling the lustful desires of the flesh. We have been born again and we live a holy life in the world. We are not of this world and we are walking in the spirit of truth. Greatness is on the inside of us.

It is, working its way to the outside of us and it is, taking us to higher levels in Him for more of the good life, Jesus came to bring us.

Know that this world is passing away and the gift of God is eternal life in Christ.

Doing the will of God is what the believer must **do in** order to have greater power in our Christian walk. Doing things correctly and right for God over and over again kills the spirit of deception in our lives every day. Walking in the spirit of truth destroys the demon spirits in your life forever.

In the book of James it is stated like this: Do ye think that the scripture saith in vain, the spirit that dewelleth in us lusteth to envy? 6 But he giveth more grace, wherefore he saith, God resisteth the proud, but giveth grace unto the humble.

7 Submit yourselves therefore to God. Resist the devil and he will flee from you. A very powerful word from God's word is flee <u>youthful</u> lust and you can walk in victory. The key is you must submit yourself unto God in order for any of His word to work in your life.

Therefore God commands us to choose life and live again in Him. To live going forward in Christ, not living backward with the devil's evil deeds or wicked works any longer. This word is a true stepping stone spoken into my life by one of my Fathers in the faith in Killeen Texas. I was stationed at Fort Hood serving in the United States Army and God sent a man of god to speak his word with power in the city of Killen. God will send a man of God into your life to speak to you. It is up to you to receive and believe the word of God that is preached.

I pray for you, to the father that we be empowered as Christians to take this word and hide it in your hearts and write it on the tables of hearts as He reveals it to you in his word, hidden truths by the Spirit in us. We have been told who the devil is and we know that there is <u>only</u> one devil in this world with many demons.

These demons are fallen angels from heaven and they are evil spirits who obey Satan. Please **do** not give into his ways anymore. We know God and we are over comers by faith and in spirit and truth, so the devil does not like **us to know God's truths and reveal those truths to others.** This is the way the devil wants you to operate. The word *"devil"* spelled backwards is the word *"lived."* God wants us to live a holy life unto Him and **do** it with in a forward progression from faith to faith and glory to glory so that you have the hope of glory in you. God is in you so feed your hope some faith and love, for you cannot **be** defeated by the devil ever again.

Remember the devil wants us to live our lives backward with him and go to hell. He wants you to go nowhere and stay in the same state his demons found you, **doing** the wrong things time after time and thinking things will get better.

The devil is a liar and things do not just get better. You must change something to get a different result. We are Children of Light and we are going to live unto our God who has put the blessing on us. We are blessed and given a new life in Christ, so we are now new creatures in Christ and old things have passed away. We spent our faith and we're waiting on our change, behold, all things have become new.

Read 2Cor 5:17 and Job 14:14

Note: Write what the Lord puts in your heart after you read the above paragraph.

_____
_____
_____
_____
_____
_____
_____
_____
_____

So give thanks unto God who is rich <u>in mercy</u> and has made you righteous. Jesus has given us the abounding grace of God. Now we know the kingdom of God has come down to us when we forget what people think of us as we **do** the will of Him who has saved us and is doing a new work in us. The greater one now lives within our hearts and the love of God is shared within all of our hearts by the Holy Ghost. We have been justified, and now we have been set aside for the Master's use to build His kingdom.

Notes:

_____
_____
_____
_____
_____
_____
_____

The Bible tells us to lay aside every weight that so easily beset us, and press onward toward the high calling which is in Christ Jesus. Let us live in peace and **do** our, Father's will so others will see and know that the God we serve has done a good work in us, and we have been made a new creatures in Christ. We are in a kingdom that will never be destroyed, because we accepted the King of Kings and Lord of Lords, who <u>reigns</u> forever and ever with us in the new life we now live.

This is a powerful truth that has made us victorious as the people of God, so you can tell the devil to go to hell without you, because you are heavenly bound. Let your voice be heard. We are overcome by the blood of the lamb and the words of our testimony, in Jesus name.

Now that you have read this study book up to this point, please write down what has been revealed to you by the Holy Spirit in your heart. Amen.

HOW TO FIGHT THE DEVIL

What battle are you going through right now? Whatever it is, don't be discouraged. The war was already won at Calvary. The battle that rages on today is a fruitless effort on the part of Satan to stop the advancement of the kingdom of God. It's an effort to keep Christians from witnessing to each other and the unsaved, and an effort; to keep Christians in their pits. It is also an effort; to make them lukewarm and not "on fire" for the things of God. Whatever battle you are going through, don't be discouraged. God is in full control. As Christians, we will endure many trials and tribulations, but rejoice because "he who is in you is greater than he who is in the world,"

(1 John 4:4) Rest easy because the victory is already ours in Christ Jesus. You are probably saying "yeah, yeah, but how do I fight the devil?" Like many people, you are either just coming out of trouble, in trouble, or about to be in trouble. Satan wants desperately to keep you in the pit. He wants to continue to keep you in financial bondage, marital strife, parental discord, work conflict, and whatever else he can do to keep you from hungering for God. So, how do we resist the schemes of the devil?

Before you can fight something, you must recognize what you are fighting. Then you must immediately prepare for the battle. The formula and plan is described in Ephesians chapter 6 verses 10-20.

This passage of scripture focuses on putting on the armor of God. Use this scripture as a constant reminder to yourself that we are not in a fight against flesh and blood but in a constant state of spiritual warfare. For we do not wrestle against flesh and blood but against principalities, against powers, against the rulers of the darkness of this age, against spiritual hosts of wickedness in the heavenly places (Eph. 6:12). But praise God! God is our shield. Take up the shield of faith, and prepare yourself to fight the wiles of the devil.

We have all prepared ourselves for a high school or college exam, a big game, or a promotion. Think about what you did to prepare for that moment. For that test, you may have put in hours and hours of study time. For the big game, your coach put you through long days and nights of practice. For that promotion, you endured numerous work challenges and dug your heels in to seek favor in your employer's eyes. Then the day comes, the moment of truth when, all your efforts will be put to the test. Think back. Did you pass every test, win every game, and get every promotion? Probably not In fact, you may have failed on numerous occasions, but be encouraged, because success often comes by way of failure.

Notes: _____
_____
_____
_____

We can apply this same logic to the spiritual battle that rages on in your life today as trouble waits. Even as you are reading this, the devil is preparing to come and immediately steal the message God has sown in your heart (Mark *4:15)* Just as you prepared for some of life's events and challenges, I encourage you to prepare for what spiritual battles await you. I encourage you to diligently seek God to guide you through the fight you are in right now. We are not perfect, but we walk in the perfection of Christ until that day we will be made perfect in Christ through our resurrected bodies. Until that glorious day of the second coming of our Lord and Savior Jesus Christ, we have to prepare and maintain our battle stance against the spiritual forces of the devil.

In Ephesians 6: 10-20, Paul is instructing us to put on the whole armor of God, and gird your waist with truth, having put on the breastplate of righteousness. Take a minute to reflect on your walk with Christ. Are you standing upright (righteous) and walking in obedience to God? This is pivotal to an effective battle stance. We must stand righteous in the sight of the Lord to receive His strength and His power, which will enable us to overcome all things. Once you have checked your battle stance, you must shod your feet with the preparation of the gospel of peace (Eph 6:15) and stand on the word of God.

Just imagine trying to walk or run on hot coals. These hot coals represent the fiery coals tossed in your path by the devil to try slow, you down while his satanic forces throw fiery darts at you. Well, there is no tactic used by the enemy capable of extinguishing the power and authority God has given us. If you stand firm on God's word and allow it to take root into your life you are prepared for the fight. So take up that battle stance and equip yourself with the word of god (your sword) and your shield of faith with which you will be able to quench all the fiery darts of the wicked one (Ephesians. 6:16) Now you are ready. God will guide you and protect you and has also given you the power to go on the offensive.

He also writes in verse 17 for us to take the helmet of salvation and the sword of the spirit, which is the word of God. The message is clear that the armor of God is not just meant to be a passive defense mechanism but rather to be used offensively against these satanic forces. If you are in a fight, you don't just pick up a sword for shown but to fight with. So let's get on the offensive and fight the devil. Jesus has given us authority over all the power of the enemy. He spoke this in, Luke 10:19, "behold, I give you the authority to trample on serpents and scorpions, and over all the power of the enemy, and nothing shall by any means hurt you."

So, now that we are spiritually alert to the fact that demonic forces are behind what comes against you to harm you, we are ready to fight the devil.

As Christians, we will be tempted and may often stumble in life. What you do to recover (that is repent) — determines what the outcome will be. In the book of James, he (James) talks about how job had to experience trials and tribulations because only through his suffering could he intimately experience and comprehend the Lord as a compassionate and merciful LORD.

Notes _____

_____

_____

_____

_____

_____

_____

_____

_____

_____

CHRISTIAN POWERFUL D-WORDS

Kingdom building **D-words** edify of all Christians as we hide the word in our hearts and speak the word. In 1 John we get the number? D- word in **DEED**.

1 John 3:18
"My little children let us not love in word, neither in tongue; but in **deed** and in truth."

1 John 3:22
And whatsoever we ask, we receive of him, because we keep his commandments, and **do** those things that are pleasing in his sight. Now we must study the text and get an understanding and mix our work with faith. We must see God work on us by faith and then through us as we **do** His will, not in words but in **deeds**.

The word says in Proverbs 18:21 that words you speak are life and death, because the word says the power of life and death is in the tongues so watch what you say and how you say it. Do a group word study and get the supporting scripture from the word of God and share within the group the importance of the words you have looked up and defined. This chapter will have just a few of the most important powerful Christian d- words for you as believers, who need to speak and keep good words in our mouth and in our hearts.

The purpose of word studies is to train your spirit man to produce words of edification to help to build your faith and speak the word. Every word we speak as Christians is powerful in the spiritual realm and works on our behalf for life or death. Now this part of the lesson will help you in knowing some of the most powerful D-words in the kingdom of God as you live this new life style.

Three things to remember from this study section of the book:

1. Know it and do it and speak these words from the heart as unto God.
2. Believe every word you speak is life or death to you and for others.
3. Be a person of the words you speak with understanding (stand on it).

The first two words of this lesson have been done for you, as a guide with the supporting scripture and D-word defined.

1. **Doctrine of Christ:** the Greek word for doctrine is *logos* which is the written word of God, Hebrews 6:1 is the foundation Christians must build on. "Therefore, leaving the principles of the **doctrine** of Christ, let us go on unto perfection; not laying again the foundation of repentance from dead works and of faith toward God." The word **"doctrine"** in this sense means instruction or teaching about God and how you live

unto Him and for Him in Christ. All the words that God gave Jesus to speak, is all His doctrine which was all that Jesus taught.

2. **Divine**: godly, godlike, a person with superhuman power that God can only give. Can God? Yes: God can, because he is God: who is supremely good and magnificent all by Himself. Every perfect and good gift comes from God the Father. 2 Peter 1:3-4 say's "According as his **divine** power hath given unto us all things that pertain unto life and godliness, through the knowledge of him that hath called us to glory and virtue: 4 Whereby are given unto us exceeding great and precious promises: that by these ye might be parkers of the **divine** nature, having escaped the corruption that is in the world through lust."

3. **Delivered:** _____

4. **Discipline:** _____

5. **Developed:** _____

6. **Devour:** _____

7. **Demonstrated:** _____

8. **Deeper:** _____

9. Depart: _____

10. Devoted: _____

11. Display: _____

12. Diligent: _____

13. Destiny: _____

14. Discernment: _____

15. Desire: _____

16. **Decided:** _____

_____

_____

_____

_____

17. **Directions:** _____

_____

_____

_____

_____

18. **Decree:** _____

_____

_____

_____

_____

19. **Declare:** _____

_____

_____

_____

_____

20. **Determined:** _____

_____

_____

_____

_____

21. **Doer:** _____

_____

_____

_____

_____

22. **Dependable:** _____

_____

_____

_____

_____

23. **Different:** _____

_____

24. **Discretion:** _____

_____

26. **Dream:** _____

_____

27. **Dwell:** _____

_____

28. **Drawnigh:** _____

_____

29. **Done:** _____

_____

30. **Descended:** _____

_____

Note that the number 33 is Jesus age, according to the bible, when he was crucified, resurrected, and departed to go to the Father. He began at age **thirty and completed all the work the father had for him to do while on earth. He did all his work in three years.**

The number three is very important because the number three in the bible <u>represents</u> "The Trinity" which means the union of three divine persons in one God, It was all done in and according to God's perfect will and divine power.

To get the most benefit from the lesson go over at least two to three words each group setting and share with one another the revelation that God has given you with the group. You may have different results, because the Spirit reveals things to us based on our spiritual maturity and understanding.

Remember that, all the words must be supported by God's word. They are to help build up the Saints and tear down the <u>devils</u> kingdom. Then and only then will you know that you have the right ammunition to fight the devil. All of <u>God's</u> kingdom D-words build His Saints up and tear down, Satan's kingdom. We are all God's helpers one to another and we are all working together to tear down the Kingdom of Darkness. So study these words in a group using two different translations of the bible, if available. Now that is good news for all God's people to study unto God. Amen.

Notes: _____

_____

_____

_____

_____

_____

_____

_____

_____

_____

_____

_____

_____

_____

_____

_____

_____

_____

_____

GOD KNOWS US AND ABOUT THEM

God talked to us while we were yet being formed in our mothers, womb. We did not understand Him so we did what we saw others do apart from God. This is why the word of God said to train up a child in the way that they should go and when they're old they will not depart from it.

1John 2:3-5 says "This how we are sure that we have come to know Him: by keeping His commands. 4. The one who says, "I have come to know Him" without keeping His commands, is a liar, and the truth is not in him. **If our claims do not correspond with His demands, then we really don't know Him, you're a liar, and the truth is not in him.** 5 But whoso keeps His Word in him verily is the Love of God perfected; hereby know we that we are in Him. God is saying for us to train our children to know all about Jesus because he is the "way maker."

That is why what you **do** will demonstrate who you will be and who you will live for. God never gives up on us, because He knows what He has placed in us and once we come to know the truth that is in Jesus we will be complete in Christ.

2 Peter 2:4 states "For if God spared not the angels who sinned. "This refers to a specific type of sin, which was actually the sin of fallen Angels cohabiting with women that took place before the Flood, and then after the Flood "[Gen.6:1-4] "But cast them down to hell," refers to Tartarus, visited by Christ after His death on the cross and immediately before His resurrection. In fact, He preached " unto the spirits in prison," which refers to the fallen angels (1 Peter 3:19-20) and delivered them into chains of darkness where they have been imprisoned to be reserved unto Judgment. This refers to the coming "Great White Throne Judgment," when they will then be cast into the Lake of Fire.

Read: [Revelation. 20-10and 19:20] and 2 Peter 2:9.

1Peter 2:11-12 states "Dearly beloved, I beseech you as strangers and pilgrims." No one is really a pilgrim in the biblical sense who has not first become a stranger to this world. "Abstain from fleshly lusts, which war against the soul" tells us that the "sin nature:" is still with us even as Christians. 12 Having your **conversation** honest among the Gentiles: that, whereas they speak against you as evildoers, they may by your good works (separated from sin), which they shall behold in the day of visitation.

So God sent Jesus for us all because He loves us and cares for us more than we will ever know. John 3:16 tell us of His great love for us. That is the reason why Jesus is the way to the Father. Jesus is the truth and the life. He is known as (the Light of the World,) and no man can come to the Father without Jesus Christ.

God has given us this understanding because we asked for it. That is why the Bible commands us, that if any man lacks wisdom let him ask of God who freely gives it and in all thy getting, get an understanding because you must stand and see God at work in your life. God reveals His truth to us day by day only when you ask in truth and in spirit, because he knows your heart. God's revelation of truth is not based on your head knowledge, so we must follow His truth it not try to think it through as some have tried to do and have failed. No man can give <u>you understanding</u> and wisdom, only God can give these things to those who ask in faith and spirit and in truth. This is why the Bible says out of the <u>abundance</u> of the heart, the mouth will speak, but your heart must be fixed on Christ before good treasures can come out of it.

Notes: _____
_____
_____
_____
_____
_____
_____
_____
_____

This is deeper than we will ever know so go deep with Christ in your heart, and let the living waters start following out of you belly. That means you need to watch what you say and think with your heart and stop using your head knowledge, which has led you down the wrong path in times past. This is why in the word it says that there is a way that seems right unto a man but the end is destruction.

Here is a revelation for you. God has placed a word in His word for us to study and he will reveal it (**them**) to us as we read and seek after him. Watch Him show you, you and tell you to come out from among them. You need not go to them and come back to Him seeking for answers. Jesus is the answer to all of your needs. Now you must be a true Christian and go to Him (Christ) and He will teach you and then send you back to them with the witness at work in you. (**The Holy Spirit is the witness**).

Let Christ in your heart by faith and He will teach you by His spirit all things. It is in Him we are who we are, truly we're in Jesus Christ our Lord and He is our Savior. God is our first love so we must love one another if we belong to God. This is not a suggestion from God for us to love each other. It is a commandment from God that we **do** this. It is so the world will know we are from Him the light of the world has been made known to them if we have love for one another.

We can have fellowship one to another with God the Father and God the Son and God the Holy Spirit because we obeyed from the heart.

Jesus did it all for us at the cross so we are able to enjoy the Christian life with God and God's people. Here is a revelation about the word bread. Jesus is known as the bread of life. We do need bread and water to live. When the Holy Spirit lead Jesus up into the mountains and he had no food to eat while he was seeking the Father. The Tempter (Satan) can unto Him with temptations. Satan said to Jesus; if thou be the Son of God turn these stones into bread. Jesus replied to Satan that man should not live by bread alone, but by ever word that proceededth out of the mouth of God.

The powerful revelation God gave me about, Jesus reply to Satan. This insight comes out of the word **bread**. For us as Christians and the New Testament Church of believers we must know the importance of being partakers of the **bread of life** as we feed hungry souls the word of God. In order to be feed with this bread you must drop the **B** off of the word **bread** and do what it says (**read**) God's word and feed the Holy Spirit what He needs, (God's word). We are living in the truth in him who has called us out of darkness into His light, to do good works by faith. You must show them you know them by your works and studying God's word which is eating the bread that you read each day, for this is our daily bread. Talk to God each day and (James 2:18 says "Yes, a man may say, you have Faith, and I have works: show me your faith without your works, and I will show you my Faith by my works. Show them your Faith and your good works and then they can tell who your God is." Amen

Luke 8: 4-12 The Parable of the "Sower"
A "Sower" went fourth sowing precious seeds (the word of God).

4 And when much people were gathered together, and were come to Him out of every city, He spoke by a parable (parables had a tendency to confuse His opposers and to enlighten those who were truly His followers) **5** A sower in this case, the Evangelist went out to sow his seed(the Word of God) and as he sowed, some fell by the way side referred to an area which had not been prepared for the seed and it was trodden down, and the fowls of the air devoured it (demon spirits). **6** And some (seed) fell upon a rock covered by a very shallow layer of soil and as soon as it was sprung up, it withered away, because it lacked moisture (water) due to the rock, the roots could not go down into the soil where the moisture was. **7** And some (seed) fell among thorns pertains to good ground, but yet the competition of the thorns would prove to be a debilitating factor; and the thorns sprang up with it, and choked it. **8** And other fell on good ground means ground that was not full of rocks or thorns and sprang up refers to bountiful growth, and bear fruit an hundredfold presents a tremendous harvest. And when He had said these things, He cried, He who has ears to hear, let him hear (many did not have "ears to hear" because their hearts were hardened; some few did, and they changed the world!).
9 And His Disciples asked Him, saying, What might this Parable be? This proclaims the story being understood perfectly well, but not its meaning.

10 And He said, unto you all who sincerely seek to know the Lord, and have a deeper understanding of His Word it is given to know the mysteries the word implies knowledge withheld; however, Jesus is saying that the scriptural significance to these mysteries is about to be revealed, at least to those who hunger and thirst after righteousness; of the Kingdom of God; but to others in Parables the Divine story would be veiled to the careless and indifferent; that seeing they might not see, and hearing they might not understand pertained to a willful blindness and a willful lack of comprehension; they had no desire to know. And you cannot show what you do not know, but you can show what you know.
11 Now the parable is this: **The seed is the Word of God**. **12** Those by the way side are they who hear; **then comes the devil, and takes away the Word out of their hearts**; he is able

to do this simply because they have little regard for the Word, lest they should believe and be saved a willful blindness resulted in a judicial blindness.

1. Sow to where you would like to go, and watch how you sow and what you sow.

2. Sow good seeds in good ground and expect a good harvest come crop time.

3. If you have sown some bad seeds pray unto God for a crop failure.
4. Remember you will reap what you sow so do what you know that's true and right from the heart.
5. Teach others to sow good seeds (God's word).

   Luke 6:38 the Good News Bible says "Give to others, and God will give to you. Indeed, you will receive a full measure, a generous helping, poured into your hands-all that you can hold. The measure you use for others is the one that God will use for you."

LET US DO WHAT WE HAVE BEEN TAUGHT....

This journey I thought began in Iraq, but the true journey began when I was a child. I came to know about the Lord at an early age, but I did not truly trust know the Lord as my personal Savior until much later. I was doing what I had been taught, at least not in its fullness. I was doing what was convenient for me. It wasn't until my "desert experience" that I came to truly know the Lord and learned that I had cheated myself out of many blessings throughout my life. I came to realize that as Christians, we are called to do what we have been taught from the beginning...To Trust in the Lord.

I was going off to fight a war. That is what I told myself the morning of January 10, 2005 which was the day I boarded a plane bound for Iraq. What awaited me was uncertainty in my heart. I was not fearful of the nature of war and the possibility of getting hurt or maybe even killed. My two main concerns were and how was I going to "eat" spiritually, and how, would my family be in my absence. I went to Iraq broken in many ways. My walk with Christ had suffered a beating at the hands of me. That's right 'me'. You see my conviction has always been, if my life was in turmoil, first look at my obedience to God in all His direction for my life. After careful evaluation, I realized why I felt so broken; I was not doing what I was taught from the beginning...Trust in the Lord with all my heart. What most people are challenged with today is complete trust in God to handle all their needs. We often trust God to do some things but figure we can handle other things on our own. God has called us to put our complete trust in Him. Proverbs 3:5 states 'Trust in the Lord with all your heart...'

"I Got You." That is what I used to tell my daughter and my son when we played the trust game. I would stand behind them and tell them to fall backwards. Don't bend your knees, or look back. Just fall back...I Got you. My daughter initially started falling back but bending her knees, looking back, trying to brace herself with her hands for a hard crash to the ground. Bracing for impact just in case I really wasn't there; as if she were thinking "what if daddy isn't paying attention; what if he doesn't catch me; that sure would hurt." I started really close to her. She would barely fall back and I would catch her. But not before several uncertain moments where she asked, "What if you don't catch me."

"Which I promptly replied, "Trust me...I Got you." So without looking back or bending her knees or trying to catch herself, she fell back and of course I caught her.

Which launched, what I call, a massive child offensive on her part wanting me to play this game over and over and over. Ah the joy of being a father. She trusted me. This simple game of trust excites my spirit as a father. Soon after, the process started all over with my son. Trust me...I Got you. This is the basic principle God brought back to my revelation during my desert experience. Simply put, He wants me to trust Him. This is the foundation for God's message for you right now. This is what our focus will be in this chapter of study. God taught us this principle from the start of our walk with Him.

Somewhere along your journey in life, you learned trust. In most cases many people learned to trust their friends or family members. As Christians, we all have stepped out in faith. It is this leap of faith where trust in our Heavenly Father was revealed to us. By repenting of our sins and asking for forgiveness, each of us have said 'Lord we trust You.' To trust is to place one's confidence in; to hope. It can also be liken to dependency. Meaning we depend on those we trust. Just as a child depends on his or her parents, Jesus has called us to that same kind of dependency or trust.

Let's examine this principle of trust a little closer.

How much should we trust in Him?

_____
_____
_____
_____
_____

Proverbs 3:5 I don't presume to say this is easy for anyone but I know it is possible for everyone. As we defined 'Trust' earlier in this chapter, it is the act of putting one's confidence in God. I often found that trust was lacking in my relationship with God. Out of my mouth would proceed 'of course I trust God' but my heart and my actions were contrary. I would say I was giving a perceived problem unto God but would take matters into my own hands to try and resolve them. You ever find yourself doing that? This next passage is clear in directing us how to learn to Trust God.

Psalms 37: 5 _____
_____
_____
_____

In this passage of scripture the Psalmist David has given us a clear and solid message of a promise from God.

What 2 things are we called to do in this passage of scripture?

_____
_____
_____

What is the promise stated here?

_____
_____
_____

God promises to give us the desires of our heart - Psalms 37:4

Our job is to trust in Him. We have to trust God to sift through the evil desires of our hearts. We have to trust God to search our heart for those desires we have that will enrich our lives as Christians and fulfill that promise. Often times, people use scripture and try to manipulate God's word to fit their circumstance. An example would be to take this simple yet powerful passage of scripture of God's promise to give unto the desires of the heart and to say God will supply every desire of your heart. But scripture teaches us that the heart is deceitful above all things. Jeremiah 17:9

So put your trust in God for if you continue on into Jeremiah 17:10 you will see God' love, grace and faithfulness to us. He alone searches our hearts and is capable of sorting out the desires of our heart, which are profitable to our soul and will enrich our lives. God is faithful to give unto every man according to his ways and the fruits of his doings. What a powerful message. God is faithful to give unto us according to our works.

When you are in trouble, praise and keep seeking God. When you have been delivered from the snares of the wicked, Praise and continue to Seek God. When you have peace and calm in your life, Praise and Seek God. Trust God with all your heart. Now that we know how much we should trust God, let's take a look at what things to give unto God.

Cast all your care upon Him. 1 Peter 5:7And my God will supply all your need according to His riches in glory by Christ Jesus. Philippians 4:19 – Wow! God is calling you and I to trust in Him with all of our heart and He will do the rest.

This act of love is beyond compare. God is faithful and just to deliver you from whatever circumstances you are in. Just give it unto Him and watch Him work. You won't be disappointed.

Take a few minutes to jot down a few things you would like to give unto the Lord. This is not a to-do list for God. Rather an outward acknowledgment on your behalf of what you will give unto to the Lord. After you have put a few things to paper, continue without looking back. I hope you took a few minutes to jot a few things down. I know that God will see your commitment to trust in Him and cast your care upon Him. Watch Him work. When you find victory in whatever situation you are confronted with, mark it off from your list and Praise God.

Jesus is calling for us to complete dependency upon Him. This is the same absolute trust and dependency a child puts in their parents to meet their every need. During His ministry Jesus teaches his disciples this basic principle of dependency and trust. Matt 18:3 "Assuredly, I say to you, unless you are converted and become as little children, you will by no means enter the kingdom of heaven."

This same scripture is supportive of this chapter's theme of Trust. Remember early in this chapter I stated that as Christians we all have stepped out in faith. It is this faith that has allowed us to trust in the word, which we have heard and believed. So, Let us do what we have been taught….Trust God, He's got you.

YOU LEARNED IT, ONLY WHEN YOU DO IT

Listen with a Spiritual ear my brothers and sisters in Christ we must come to the real truth of what we say we have learned. Let us take a look into the word of God and study this process that works by us operating in faith. God's word is telling us to learn, in whom you have confessed your belief in. Christ is going to develop us from within. Once we have learned the things Christ has taught us in His name we must confess what we want to possess. Let's take a look. What does the word learn really mean? God has revealed this to me and I would like to pass it on to the body of Christ.

Learn: to gain knowledge, comprehension, or mastery of through experience or study to memorize, possessing systematic knowledge. Now one key word that stands out in the definition of learn is knowledge and this knowledge comes from God and it is the knowledge of Him who has called you out of darkness. John 8:12 Jesus said "12 Then Jesus spoke to them again, saying, "I am the light of the world. He who follows Me shall not walk in darkness, but have the light of life.""

Proverbs 1:7 "the fear of the Lord is the beginning of knowledge but fools despise wisdom and instruction."

Proverbs 4:7 "wisdom is the principal, thing; therefore get wisdom, and with all thy getting get understanding." The word knowledge is the state or fact of knowing; familiarity, awareness, or understanding gained through experience or study. I will paraphrase what God has commanded us in 2 Timothy 15, to study to show yourself approved unto God. Take a minute to read that verse in your bible now before your continue on with this lesson. Now with the word Knowledge we can take out the word know in biblical definition means to have learned that which in truly known to the truth. This is to have experience of, possessing special or secret information that you must share with others and then they will know you have learned the word of God from the Holy one, that's in your heart and you are doing what have learned from the Father.

Ephesians 4: 20-24

But ye have not so learned Christ; 21 If so be that ye have heard him, and have been taught by him, as the truth is in Jesus: 22 That you put off concerning the former conversation the old man, which is corrupt according to the deceitful lusts; 23 And be renewed in the spirit of your mind; 24 And that ye put on the new man, which after God is created in righteousness and true holiness.

As we continue the lesson it is important that you write notes to yourself and start sharing your wisdom and knowledge that God will give unto you as you just do it.

I know you thought Nikee came up with the words "JUST DO IT" but that was and is in God's word for all the believers to just do it and follow the word out and not to think in out. Stop and read **Isaiah 55:6-11** about our thoughts.

You must understand you want to know it now, and the now is in the k**now** which is in the knowledge that begins with the fear of the LORD and the knowledge is in Him. We must know this in our hearts and **follow Him** to get out. That's why we must just do it, and walk in what we say we know right now. Remember Satan is busy and just because you know it does not mean you will do it. Jesus said to Peter in the book of John chapter 21 "Feed My Sheep" **John 21:19** "This He spoke, signifying by what death he would glorify God. And when He had spoken this, He said to him, "Follow Me."

But you must do what you say you know and be justified in Him by faith and through your obedience. The bible is clear to us who walk in the spirit which is the word of God. Jesus said that the words that He speaks are spirit and life and **Proverbs 18-21**also tells us where the power is. Please read proverbs 18-21 and then continue the lesson.

And in the book of James chapter 1 verse 2-7 it reads 2 "My brethren, count it all joy when you fall into various trials, 3 knowing that the testing of your faith produces patience. 4 But let patience have its perfect work, that you may be perfect and complete, lacking nothing. 5 If any of you lacks wisdom, let him ask of God, who gives to all liberally and without reproach, and it will be given to him. 6 But let him ask in faith, with no doubting, for he who doubts is like a wave of the sea driven and tossed by the wind. 7 For let not that man suppose that he will receive anything from the Lord; 8 he is a double-minded man, unstable in all his ways. To him who knows to do right and does not it is sin in the book of James. So then others will see that what you do is truly based on you say you know and who you say you know will show up in what you do. As we begin to study the word learn in its fullness I hope and pray that your eyes can be enlightened to a powerful truth that provokes you to do what you have learned. Now we can see it and hid it, in our hearts once the spirit gets feed this fresh revaluation you will do greater things and have a good understanding of the bible.

1 Corinthians 2:13-16 13 These things we also speak, not in words which man's wisdom teaches but which the Holy Spirit teaches, comparing spiritual things with spiritual. 14 But the natural man does not receive the things of the Spirit of God, for they are foolishness to him; nor can he know them, because they are spiritually discerned.15 But he who is spiritual judges all things, yet he himself is rightly judged by no one. 16 For "who has known the mind of the Lord that he may instruct Him?" But we have the mind of Christ. Once your spirit has been taught by the Holy Spirit, expressing spiritual truths in spiritual words you will be able to walk in what you have learned.

2 Timothy 3:15-16
And that from a child thou **hast known the holy scriptures**, which are able to make you wise for salvation through faith in Christ Jesus. All scripture is given by inspiration of God, and is profitable for doctrine, for reproof, correction, for instruction in righteousness: We must always remember to apply this word in our Christian walk and live it out for God and show them you know Him.

Remembering to walk in the word and apply it to how we should now be living as believers who know the truth. Jesus is the truth and the way out of all who believe the word of God. Now; once we add ed, to the word learn it then becomes what we have learned: that equates to what we should be doing, if we say we have learned it. We now have the mind of Christ, because we're doing what we say we have learned in Christ. The word says in 1John 2:3 "Now by this we know that we know Him, if we keep His commandments. 4 He who says, "I know Him" and does not keep His commandments, is a liar, and the truth is not in him. 5 But whoever keeps His word, truly the love of God is perfected in him. By this we know that we are in Him. 6 He who says he abides in Him ought himself also to walk just as He walked. And Jesus also stated all men will know that you know Him, if you have love for one another just as I have loved you. So we must not just be a hearer of the word only but hearers and doers of the word in love from the heart. Please listen with the ear in your heart and use the ear in what you have learned in Christ and do what the word say's do to the glory of God. All Saints should go about doing good works in Christ once they have learned Christ from the heart.

Joshua gives us some instructions to follow; read and study Joshua 1:8.

Joshua 1:8

"Do not let this Book of the Law depart from your mouth; meditate on it day and night, so that you may be careful to do everything written in it. Then you will be prosperous and successful.

John 5:19-21

"Then answered Jesus and said unto them, Verily, verily, I say unto you, The Son can do nothing of himself, but what he seeth the Father do: for what things so ever he doeth, these also doeth the Son likewise.

For the Father loveth the Son, and sheweth him all things that himself doeth:
and he will shew him greater works than these, that ye may marvel.

For as the Father raiseth up the dead, and quickeneth them; even so the Son quickeneth whom he will." what is Jesus telljg us in these scriptures and how can we apply this to our - life? **Notes:** Here is a good key note from the author Evangelist Griffin, remember more is caught than taught. So watch what you do and do what is right from your heart at all times because your children and family and friends are watching what you are doing and they will catch what they see and not as much as what you teach or preach. So preach and teach to everybody you meet and say something if you have too. Live your Life out and keep shouting it out everywhere you go, let the redeemed of the Lord say so, in Jesus name.

James 1:21-25 —read and study this text.

"Therefore, get rid of all moral filth and the evil that is so prevalent and humbly accept the word planted in you, which can save you.

Do not merely listen to the words, and so deceive yourselves. Do what it says anyone who listens to the word but does not do what it says is like a man who looks at his face in a mirror and, after looking at himself, goes away and immediately forgets what he looks like, but the man who looks intently into the perfect law that gives freedom, and continues to do this, not forgetting what he has heard, but doing it — he will be blessed in what he does."

Note this: with this being said to us and as you read it, write down what your spirit man was saying to you.

Acts 20:32

"Now I commit you to god and to the word of his grace, which can build you up and give you an inheritance among all those who are sanctified." let us do god's will, which we know <u>is, God's</u> word and, live the life god intended for us to live forever with him." just do it and you will see <u>God's</u> hand is at, work in your life acting on what you say you believe: now that you believe in God's word. Now that is good news and the gospel that we preach Christ and not ourselves.

KNOWING WHO I AM IN CHRIST

This is probably one of the greatest things the Devil tries to have from a person once they give there live to Christ. Being a babe in Christ a lot of times people don't have a lot of knowledge about Jesus and who they are in Christ. The most important thing to them is that they were lost and now they are found. That sin was a shackle that kept them in bondage but by the Grace of God in Jesus Christ they are saved form Sin and the wrath to come upon all who continue to "willfully Sin".

But it is crucial to **Know who you are in Christ**. Through the Salvation Jesus freely gives us we change to become the Children of God. **Galatians 5:17-1917. Therefore if any man be in Christ, he *is* a new creature: old things are passed away; behold all things are become new. 18 And all things are of God, who hath reconciled us to himself by Jesus Christ, and hath given to us the ministry of reconciliation; 19. To wit, that God was in Christ, reconciling the world unto himself, not imputing their trespasses unto them; and hath committed unto us the word of reconciliation.**

Even though God has created every man because of sin our relationship was broken but through Jesus it has been restored and Jesus dwells in us by Faith. The only way, we can find out who we are in Christ is study the Scriptures and allow the Holy Spirit to lead us according to God instructions. New Christians are like little Children, they guidance and direction by others that are of full age in Christ. One of the most important ministries of the Church is to Nature new Christians.

Let take a look at some things that identify us with Christ.

1. You are **crucified with Christ. Read Galatians 2:20.** As you study this scripture let the Holy Spirit open your understanding to what it really means to be crucified with Christ. This is not only something that must happen when you are born again but must continue to happen on a daily basis.

Notes: _____
_____
_____
_____
_____
_____
_____

2. You are a **"victor" in Jesus Christ**. That victory is us overcoming the damnation of Sin through the blood of our Lord and Savior Jesus Christ. Jesus gave us the Victory at Calvary when he conquered Death, Hell, and the Grave.

Read 1 Corinthians 15: 47-58.

Notes: _____
_____
_____
_____
_____

3. Your have become the **Light of the World and the Salt of the Earth**. What does this really mean? **Read Mathew 5:13-16.** This really brings out who Jesus says we are in Him and what he expect of us as believers. He did save us and leave us here to hide our Faith but to let be seen of others.

Notes: _____
_____
_____
_____
_____

4. You are the **Righteous of God in Christ Jesus**. Hold it! You say. I don't know about this righteous thing. That's right, Righteous **in Christ Jesus.** Not in ourselves but in Christ we are to be Righteous. **Read Ephesians 4:23-32.**

Notes: _____
_____
_____
_____
_____

5. You are dead to Sin but **Alive unto God through Christ**. Well what doesn't really mean to be dead to sin? This is simply denying the nature of Sin that dwells in the flesh and surrendering to your new nature which is in Jesus. Some might say, well what actually is my new nature in Christ? Simply put to be conformed in the image of Jesus. **Read Roman 1:1-14**

Notes: _____
_____
_____
_____
_____

6. You have just become a **Soldier**. You say what, A Soldier! Yes, that is right a Soldier in the Lord's Army. As a Christian you have just enlisted to fight against the forces of Hell. Satan and all his host will try and prevail over you but they are defeated foes. Endure the hardships and tough times that lay ahead. You will prevail in Christ. **Read 2 Timothy 1:1-4**

Notes: _____

7. You are one of **God's Elect**. Some say what does it really mean to be God's elect? To simply put it we have been elected by God through the plan of Salvation, which is in Jesus, to be heirs of his Kingdom. What a great thing to know that God elected you to become one of his children by faith in Christ. **Read Romans 8: 28-39**

Notes: _____

8. You are one of **God Redeemed**. You have escaped the judgment of Sin. Who are those that have been redeemed? All that have believed in the Lord Jesus Christ as their personnel Savior. That's right! Everyone that has been born again of the blood of Jesus Christ has redeemed from the curse of the Sin. **"Set Free" Read Galatians 3:6-18**

Notes: _____

9. You are a **New Creature**. If any man be in Christ he is a new creature: old things are passed away; behold all things have become new. **2 Corinthians 5:17** You say well I

look like the same old person. This is fact you do to a certain degree. You still live in this same flesh body but the man inside will be different. He will be changed into the image of Jesus. No longer any more! The old man will die daily in order for the man in Christ to live.

Notes: _____
_____
_____
_____
_____
_____

10. You are the **Blessed of God. Ephesians 1: 3-6** teaches us that we are blessed of God through our Lord and Savior Jesus Christ. Jesus has gives us all spiritual blessing in heavenly places. God has so many blessing in store for us because he loves us. He has given us the keys to his kingdom and the blessing in this life until we come into the fullness of his presence for ever. Read Genesis 1, Psalms 1, 64, 65, 66, 94, Isaiah 56, Revelations 1, 19, let the Holy Spirit Speak to you through these messages.

Notes: _____
_____
_____
_____
_____
_____

WE HAVE MORE "POWER" THAN THE DEVIL

This is a concept that most Christians have a hard time excepting. I don't know what is so much easier to except being saved by the blood of Jesus than to except by his stripes we are healed. The bible teaches that we walk by faith and not by sight. That also includes feelings. Sometimes we might not feel saved or sanctified but we have to remember it is not by what we feel is by faith. I know it did feel good when Jesus took the nails in his hands and feet for us but it was necessary that the world could be saved through him. Just as we except Christ as our Savior we must also be willing except the power of the Holy Ghost that gives us the victory over Satan. Let's examine what the Lord says about this **power**.

Matthew 10:1 And when he (Jesus) had called unto *him* his twelve disciples, he gave them power *against* unclean spirits, to cast them out, and to heal all manner of sickness and all manner of disease.

Notes: _____
_____
_____
_____
_____
_____
_____
_____
_____

Jesus gave the disciples this power against the devil and all other demonic spirits. as we study the word of god we see Jesus commissioned his disciples to go as messengers of God. Once we are saved we also become messengers and disciples for Christ. **Acts 1:8 but ye shall receive power, after that the Holy Ghost is come upon you: and ye shall be witnesses unto me both in Jerusalem, and in all Judea, and in Samaria, and unto the uttermost part of the earth**; This power that Jesus gives us to equip the saints to be witness everywhere we and go and through all things we do. Jesus worked miracles through the apostles by faith and he will also work them today through believers today by faith. This power is the spirit of Christ working in us. The closer we walk with the lord in our faith the more he will reveal unto us.

Notes: _____
_____
_____
_____
_____

It takes certain situations in our lives to build our faith. Just as the disciples said to Jesus "lord increase our faith. We must also cry out with an earnest desire for our faith to be increased. Sometimes we don't like the direction God send us in order for it to be increased. If we didn't have problems in life how would we know that Jesus is the answer? I can recall many times in my walk with the lord earnestly praying for different things. Some of those prayers were answered with divine miracles and others were answered in ways I didn't expect. There was a specific time I remember a couple in our church had a new born baby with a hole in its heart. They rushed the baby to a specialist in another state to operate. The church began to pray for this child and the night before surgery during prayer meeting there was a great burden for this child. We began to gather around the altar and reach out to the lord for a miracle. The next morning just before surgery the doctor conducted one final x-ray and examination before surgery. Amazed at his findings the heart was completely healed. The little girl is healthy and as normal any other child today. **The fervent effectual prayers of the righteous man availleth much; there is power in prayer!**

During my deployment to Iraq I witnessed many answered prayers and seen the power of god transform the hearts and lives of soldiers and civilians. I can recall a specific time when one of our convoy's were on a mission to visit one of the local schools being built. The policy was not to let civilian vehicles to close to the convoy. While in route there was a vehicle that approached the rear of the convoy at a high rate of speed flashing his lights and trying to get them to stop. The rear gunner advised that before he engaged the vehicle he had a gut feeling this person was trying to tell them something and not to inflict harm. He radioed the convoy commander and advised him of the situation. A decision was made and to stop and find out what he wanted. An interpreter was with the convoy to relay the information given. After all was said and done the person worked for the Iraqi police but was not in a police car. He warned them of an ambush that was set up on an over pass just several miles away. This is just another example of god's mercy and power watching over us. **Psalms 150:1. Praise ye the lord. Praise god in his sanctuary: praise him in the firmament of his power. 2. Praise him for his mighty acts: praise him according to his excellent greatness. (King David was I witness to the might acts of god's mercy and power. he delivered him out of King Saul's hand and the hands of many others who were his enemies.)**

Notes: _____
_____
_____
_____
_____
_____

Let's take a look at the power that Jesus has bestowed upon the church today.

Mark 16:15-18 and he said unto them, go ye into all the world and preach the gospel to every creature 16.He that believeth and is baptized shall be saved; but he that believeth not shall be damned.17. And these signs shall follow them that believe; in my name shall they cast out devils; they shall speak with new tongues; 18 They shall take up serpents; and if they drink any deadly thing, it shall not hurt them; they shall lay hands on the sick, and they shall recover.

Comments: (we see here that Jesus commissioned his disciples to go and preach the gospel into all the world. i took the power of god working in them in order for them to have the boldness to speak the name of Jesus after seeing him crucified on the cross. but after he had risen they knew he had the keys to death, hell, and the grave. Jesus told them they would be signs that followed believers. Many people will try and say well that was just for the disciples but Jesus said "them that believe" that includes all believers that will exercise this power given in the name of Jesus.)

Notes: _____
_____
_____
_____
_____
_____
_____
_____
_____
_____

Philippians 4:13 I can do all things through Christ who strengthens me.

Comments: (the apostle Paul taught and ministered the word of God to the Philippian Church. They had a heart to give to furtherance of the gospel. Paul encouraged them to know no matter what state they were in god would supply all of their needs. They were to keep their eyes on Christ and to know it is him that strengthen them or empower them to be used for the glory of God.)

2 Peter 1:3 according as his divine power hath given unto us all things that pertain unto life and godliness, through the knowledge of him that hath called us to glory and virtue: 4. Whereby are given unto us exceeding great and precious promises; that by these ye might be partakers of the divine nature, having escaped the corruption that is in the world through lust. 5. And besides this, giving all diligence, add to your faith virtue; and to virtue, knowledge 6. And to knowledge, temperance; and to temperance, patience;

and to patience, godliness; 7. And to godliness, brotherly kindness; and to brotherly kindness, charity. 8. For if these things be in you, and abound, they make you that ye shall neither *be* barren nor unfruitful in the knowledge of our Lord Jesus Christ. 9. But he that lacketh these things is blind, and cannot see afar off, and hath forgotten that he was purged from his old sins. 10. Wherefore the rather, brethren, give diligence to make your calling and election sure: for if ye do these things, ye shall never fall:

Comments: (the apostle Peter tells us of this power here in 2 Peter. The Lord gives shows us here that the power to love like God and to be the express image of Jesus Christ our lord and Savior only come through the power of God working in us.

Notes: _____

_____

_____

_____

_____

_____

_____

_____

Read and study the following scriptures.

1. 1 Corinthians 2 chapter
2. 2 Timothy 3 chapter
3. Hebrews 1 chapter
4. Psalms 147:1-7
5. 2 Corinthians 13:1-5
6. 1 Thessalonians 1:1-8
7. Acts 4:7-10
8. Act 1:1-8
9. Romans 5:1-6

Jesus has empowered you from on high to overcome the wicked one "the devil" so walk upright and exercise the power of God in your daily Christian walk. Remember: <u>"no weapon formed against you will ever prosper, so obey from the heart God's word for new life in Christ."</u>

WHO IS YOUR FATHER?

This is a question: unfortunately that can't be answered in today society for many people. God created us through a man and a woman. (Genesis Chapter 1 & 2

teaches about the creation of man and woman.) But many in today's society have taken out of context God's plan for the family and the way he originally ordained it to be. I truly believe a lot of today's problems have risen to the level they are because man has taken things into his own hands without seeking God's direction.

This has never been in God's plan for one parent to raise their children one of easiest ways he teaches us that is he did allow one parent to have the ability to reproduce children without the opposite sex.

We see the first woman: Eve: was given to Adam to be a help mate. God blessed their marriage. That's right marriage. Adam and Eve were husband and wife. Genesis 3:20 And Adam called his wife name Eve; because she was the mother of all living." They were married by God himself the creator of mankind. It is amazing how God desires to reveal himself to us as our Heavenly Father. As you continue to read the book of Genesis, you will see that what most children do sometime in their life. That is to disobey. All disobedience to God is sin. We know this word that brings much hardship, anguish, and grief to man just as it does to God. God had to punish his children: just as we have to do the same today for correction.

Hebrews 12:5-7 / 5. And ye have forgotten the exhortation which speaketh unto you as unto children, my son, despise not thou the chastening of the Lord, nor faint when thou art rebuked of him, 6. For whom the Lord loveth he chasteneth, and scourgeth every son whom he receiveth.7. If ye endure chastening, God dealeth with you as with sons; for what son is he whom the father chasteneth not?

But if ye be without chastisement, whereof all are partakers, then are ye bastards, and not sons.

Thanks, be unto God he is a God of mercy and full of compassion. It is his desire to show us the peace that passes all understanding. This is to teach us and be willing to reconcile us back to himself as dear, children.

Why is correction necessary?

We see in God's Word because of Adam's sin, all mankind entered into sin and was born with a sin nature. That is where Jesus Christ our Lord and Savior came in to the Master Plan of God. He was to be our Reconciler back to God. His Blood he shed on Calvary's cross was to be the ultimate payment for our sins that we could be forgiven by believing that he is the Son of God and that his blood washes away our sins. In all reality the only way you can become true children of God and call him father is through his Son Jesus. How can parenting your children the way God advises us to do. This can be is helpful to you as a Christian and a parent?

We are going to take a look at some reasons why it is important to know who your father is: naturally and spiritually. Children need the Joy of their fathers. There is something special about a father's <u>love,</u> just as it is about a mother's joy for her children. Neither can be replaced by the other: and one is not truly sufficient without the other. God's plan was for children to have a, father. This joy given by a father is different in many facets. God appointed the man to be the spiritual head of the home and it is his job to be the leader, director, and provider of his family.

Joy which is often rendered by the father is needed just as much as the tender and gentler joy which is usually given by the mother. This is not to say it shouldn't work both ways: but because of the makeup of men and women: it just holds true. There must be a balance between both and rendered by both.

Make no mistake about it every child wants to be embraced, cared for, feel wanted, and to have their, needs met a joy is the biggest part of the union and love is the greatest part that most, parents provide. God doesn't want children to be more favorable toward one parent than the other: and that is exactly why each parent must use the attributes given by God to nurture and rear the children up in the very admonition of Christ.

Just as in Genesis **1,** God created us in his image: we also bear the image of our earthly, father and mother. This is one of the signatures of God passed down through every person. No matter how disappointed our children <u>sometimes </u>make us: we still love them and will forgive them of their doings. God is much the same way. But we must repent of wrongdoings and come to him seeking his forgiveness that we can be in right standings with him.

(Jeremiah 31:3 —"The LORD hath appeared of old unto me, *saying,* Yea, I have loved thee with an everlasting love: therefore with loving- kindness have I drawn thee.")

One of the greatest scriptures of all John 3: 16, demonstrates our heavenly fathers love for us. Complete the lesson by describing some ways you feel in your heart and know God's <u>joy </u>toward you and how God's <u>love </u>can be demonstrated through you with joy. And you start giving thanks unto the Lord and walk upright and just in God's ways in faith.

2. Every child desires time with their, father. Time is one of the most precious commodities there is, especially in today's society. We as parents often have time to get things ready in order to successfully complete another day on the job but that is about it. That is one of the terrible things fathers have done and that is to allow the things of everyday life to replace the quality time needed so desperately with their children. It is one thing to tell your children how much you care about them and how much you are interested in their lives and fail to demonstrate it by actions.

Often we do the same things with God. We are his children and we make the same mistake so many times, very much the same way we do with our children. We sing "with great joy about **how we love Jesus"** and how we are Christians but we fail to spend time with our Heavenly Father. We wonder why we are not in his perfect will and why things doesn't seem to be getting better in our relationship with him. The answer is just that we don't spend time ° desperately needed with HIM.

If Jesus is our Lord and Savior, always spent time with the Father in prayer.

How much more should we spend time in prayer also this is simply talking to him and sharing our every care, thought, and need. Some would say why should we do this? God already knows our every need. Well this is just as we also know the every need of our earthly children and they still ask for those things.

Jesus teaches us many great lessons and here in the book of Luke is a very powerful truth. **Luke 11:9 "And I say unto you, Ask, and it shall be given you; seek, and ye shall find; knock, and it shall be opened unto you." What are some ideas you think would give you more time with GOD? And he is it really so important to spend time in his presence?**

Our Heavenly Father not only shows us the ay but also "encourages as" all the say.

Encouragement is something we need very often in our Christian walk. We face a world full of discouragement. With every turn we see how in is turning things upside down and destroying people's lives. That's why it is important to build one another in the most holy faith. The adversary is trying to discourage us, and he places other people in our life to discourage us. In **Psalms 139:3**: the Lord tells us that he is familiar with all our ways. After all: he did make us and give us life. All throughout God's Word we see many different scriptures that give us hope to continue in the faith that leads to eternal life. It is very important to apply this principle of **encouragement** daily in our lives toward our children, sisters, brothers, mothers, fathers; and friends. Encouragement is one of the most important gifts we can give to our fellow man.

This also means to assist in whatever way necessary to help others along this walk of, life. A parent to a child knows it is very crucial to encourage that child to develop his or her character and self-esteem. The Bible teaches us that LIFE and DEATH is in the tongue. God wants us to use the small member of the body to build up and not tear down. That doesn't mean not to discipline our children: but to teach them and build them according to the teaching of Jesus Christ this comes in many different lessons and from many different situations.

What I would like to do is to take some, scriptures in the word and let you ask the holy spirit to open your heart to receive the divine understanding on how to apply this principle of **encouragement** in your daily walk with Christ keep in mind, there is no situation or problem that god's word doesn't have an answer for. You ought to leap for joy knowing God has made away regardless of the way things appear.

Philippians 4:4 rejoice and again I say rejoice.

Romans 8 3 8-39 for i am persuaded, that neither, death, nor life, nor angels, nor principalities, nor powers, nor things present, nor things to come, nor height, nor depth, nor any other creature, shall be able to separate us from the love of god, which is Christ Jesus our lord."

Ephesians 4:30 — 'and grieve not the holy spirit of god, hereby ye are sealed unto the day of, redemption.'

1 Samuel 30:6 — 'and David was greatly distressed for the people spoke of stoning him, because the soul of all the people was grieved, every man for his sons and for his daughters: but David encouraged, himself in the Lord his God."

Mathew 6:31-33 — "Therefore take no thought, saying, what shall we eat? Or, what shall we drink? Or, Wherewithal shall we be clothed? (For after all these things do the Gentiles seek for your heavenly Father knoweth what ye have need of all these things. But seek ye first the kingdom of God, and his righteousness; and all these things shall be added unto you.

Jeremiah 29:11— "For I know the thoughts that I think toward you, saith the LORD, thoughts of peace, and not of evil, to give you an expected end. Then shall ye call upon me, and ye shall go and pray unto me, and I will hearken unto you. And ye shall seek me, and find me, when ye shall search for me with all your heart."

John 17:21 That they all may be one; as thou, Father, art in me, and Tin Is this entire thee, that they also may be one in us: that the world may believe that thou hast sent me. And the glory which thou gayest me I have given them; that they may be one, even as we are one: I in them, and thou in me, that they may be made perfect in one; and that the world may know that thou hast sent me, and hast loved them, as thou hast loved me.

Notes: _____
_____
_____
_____
_____
_____
_____

Our Father promises **us** protection read **Psalm 91** if we walk in the path way He has set before **US** and stay in His secret place. We must never let go of the Father's unchanging Hand, this relationship must never end, now that we know more about Him we must never let go his hand.

Psalm 121
1 I raise my eyes toward the mountains. Where will my help come from? **2** My help comes from the LORD, the maker of heaven and earth. **3**He will not allow your foot to slip; your Protector will not slumber. **4** Indeed, the Protector of Israel does not slumber or sleep. **5** The LORD protects you; the Lord is a shelter right by your side. **6** The sun will not strike you by day or the moon by night. **7** The LORD will protect you from all harm; He will protect your life. **8** The LORD will protect your coming and going both now and forever. Amen....

JUST DO THE DEED

You need to know that God is in the **doing** and hearing of His word and not in just hearing of His word. The bible is very clear and God has commanded us not just to be hearers of the word deceiving <u>ourselves,</u> but be ye **doers** of the word.

1 John 2:15 "Love not the world, neither the things that are in the world. If any man loves the world, the love of the Father is not in Him." The "world" spoken of here by John pertains to the ordered system of which Satan is the head. God the Father will not share the love that must go exclusively to Him with the world.

ST. JOHN 15:5 tells us that we do nothing without **Him. (Jesus)**
I am the vine, ye are the branches: He that abideth in me, and I in Him, the same bringeth forth much fruit: for without me ye can do nothing." So you as a Christian must now hear what the spirit is telling you to do and be fruitful in the kingdom of God. **(Matthew 7:12)** tells us; do what you want to men, what you want done unto you.
"Therefore all things whatsoever ye would that men should do to you, do ye even so to them: for this is the law and the prophets." In the book of Acts chapter 9:6 Paul had to do what the Lord said verse 6 And he trembling and astonished said he was stupefied and astounded, Lord, what will you have me to **DO**? This constitutes the moment that Paul was saved; "And the Lord said unto him, Arise, and go into the city, and it shall be told you what you must **do**" this pertains to the plan of God for Paul, which in effect would change the world.

With that being said, beware of the false prophets read and study **Matthew 7:15-29** and ask God for understanding in this area of your Christian walk so you will do good in His sight, because there are many deceivers out there. I call them **(UFO's)** unknown fools out there. **Proverbs 10:18** states "He that hideth hatred with lying lips, and he that uttereth a slander, is a fool." **(Proverbs 10:8)** "The wise in heart will receive commandments: but a prating fool shall fall." So remember that God has already painted the picture and we're in it. Now the only way you will be able to see the picture is for us to be <u>developed</u> in His word and then and only then He will manifest Himself unto us in all our **deeds**. We must stop thinking we need to be delivered from everything, and know that God has already sent the deliverance. Once we have accepted Jesus we're delivered from our sins, now He want us to be <u>developed</u> in our thinking and walk in the word of God, then we can walk in the deliverance already in us and we will never worry about going back to the old way we once walked. Amen, now that is good news.

As Christians confess, commit, confirm, conceive, and walk in the word of God being fully persuaded, that He who has promise is able and faithful to all His promises until the day of Christ return. We are now walking by the faith that we have been called into by God's saving grace and mercy. Obey the word of God and you will be transformed and people will know that you're a child of the KING of Kings and LORD of Lords. Let your light shine and walk in the light and keep the Devil under your feet. Be ready to fellowship with God in the spirit and pray at all times, never giving up, God said He will never leave us nor forsake us. So **do the deed** and keep hope alive as God moves you from faith to faith in Him with great power. Let the power of God work in you for life, and He will give you His peace that surpasses all understanding. Begin to pray and ask God to empower you more and more each day.

True Christians are followers of Jesus Christ, one who belongs to Christ. Christians that commit themselves to being Christ like and become increasingly more powerful in obeying and doing the will of God. We trust Jesus Christ by the spirit to guide our decisions, actions, and improve our attitudes. The name Christian was apparently used first by pagans to ridicule Jesus's followers, but it became a label for Christians to wear proudly.

Now let us read and study as Christians: (ACTS 11:26-28) (1 PETER 4:12-16) (1 PETER 51-11)
Notice that **Romans 10:9-17** never mentions what we think, but rather what we believe in our hearts. Faith must be used to obtain revelation from God in a pure heart. Our whole life, we need our faith to be at work while our hearts are a growing rate with God's word no matter what people say. Be pleasing to God and He will give you favor with man, once we grow we will be able to go and do the deed, and God wants to enlarge our hearts so that we can believe that the mountains, in our lives will be moved.

Most people want God to enlarge their head knowledge and walk around, just thinking they are blessed of the Lord. But with the pure heart and trusting in His word you will know you got the blessing on you. People with a lot of head knowledge cannot go far in the Kingdom of God and the people with heart knowledge can advance in the Kingdom of God. Now this is because we do our works from within on the inner man (spirit man) but not by just quoting the bible, it must be lived from the heart. **Proverb 14: 6-7** A mocker seeks wisdom and doesn't find it, but knowledge [comes] easily to the perceptive. 7 Stay away from a foolish man; you will gain no knowledge from his speech. From their head knowledge, they say things out of order and it does not line up with the word of God.

And when the squeeze is on, nothing comes out of their heart but wick pots and lie's no life; they are not living anything. They have dead faith wherein they simply believe and tremble, which is no more than what the Devil does anyway. They end up ship wrecked, and with nothing but a big head. So the proof of whether it is an education in the head and not a revelation of the heart, comes because we know more than what we are able to do. God is not impressed with what we just know and do not do. He looks for our good works in Christ by faith and He mixes it with His super natural powers so that He can move in us and work on our behalf for His glory. Because faith and works must go together and it moves the hand of God in our lives, God's spirit is working in us both to will and do of His good pleasure.

(James 2:18) tells us, "Yea. A man may say, thou hast faith, and I have works: shew me thy faith without thy works, and I will shew thee my faith by my works." A lot of people only have the belief right, but not their behavior or corresponding actions do not line up to what they believe. Faith is obeying the word of God which can really be called trusting in the unseen, in God who works in the unseen and applying some action with it. It is not just what we know, but what believe in that helps us to grow more and more. God needs you to let your faith go to work, and for us to just do the deed. He will show up and show out like He always does with power on our behalf. God is at work and we know He controls all things and He is in all things seen and unseen all for his glory and we must tell His story.

ROMANS 3:19-20

"Now we know that what things soever the law saith, it saith to them who are under the law: that every mouth may be stopped, and the world may become guilty before God. 20 Therefore by the **deeds** of the law there shall no flesh be justified in his sight: for by the law is the knowledge of sin."

Read and study **Romans 3:21-31** to give you more faith in your Christian walk. Pray unto God for more power in your spirit with Him to go to next level.

Write your prayer and pray it unto God:

_____

_____

_____

_____

_____

_____

_____

_____

_____

_____

THE WAY IN OR AWAY IN

The way in must be known by all Christians as followers of Christ, Jesus and the <u>children</u> of God. Satan knows away in deeds, and both God and Satan need a body to do their will and live in the earth. Yes, they are both spirits that need Away in or "The way in."

Genesis 6:12-14 "And God looked upon the earth, and behold, it was corrupt; for all flesh had <u>corrupted</u> his way upon the earth." 13 And God said unto Noah, the end of all flesh is come before me; for the earth is filled with violence through them; and behold, I will destroy them with the earth. 14 Make thee an ark of gopher wood; rooms shalt thou make in the ark, and shalt pitch it within and without with pitch. When God used Noah he was setting up the way in, God can only use an obeying spirit and a body that is willing to follow the truth.

Genesis 6:22 "thus did Noah; according to all that God <u>commanded</u> him, so did he." so you see, it starts with God giving us a command and us obeying the commandments of God. Every word God speaks is a command for us to obey and do for life in Him. Now here is the revelation God reveals in you being used by Gods and to be one of His children in the kingdom of God. You must do it the way He has already ordained and provided in His word for His kingdom and His glory.

The word of God is the will of God for your life, so stay in the word of God and you will be in the will of God. And His word needs to be in you, working out of you in deeds (doing). Those that God saves, He always gives us some instruction to follow. And once you come to know Him in the person of Jesus Christ, who is the way and the truth, God can now show us the way in Him. In the beginning, when God told Noah to make the ark, He told him the way he needed to make the ark.

Genesis 6:15-16
"And this is the way you are to make it: the length of the ark shall be 300 cubits, its breadth 50 cubits, and its height 30 cubits (that is, 450 ft. x 75 ft. x 45 ft.). you shall make a roof or window (a place for light) for the ark and finish it to a cubit (at least 18 inches) above and the door of the ark you shall put in the side of it; and you shall make it with lower, second, and third stories." read and study genesis chapter 6 and see how God provided the way in by using Noah and his family, to stay in the earth by Noah obeying God and <u>doing</u> what God commanded and instructed. Write what the spirit is saying unto you, after reading and thinking on this lesson this far. Follow your heart in spirit and in truth. Now Satan comes in when we walk in disobedience. **Your way out is to go back to "The way in (Jesus) and repent for your sin and He will let you in back in."**

Notes: _____

_____

_____

_____

Romans 5:19

The Expositor bible states "For as by one man's **disobedience** many were made sinners, many referred to all so by the **obedience** of one now in this text the obedient unto death, even the death of the Cross (Philippians 2:8) shall many be made righteous; and many refers to all who believe in the finished work of Jesus at the Cross.

Romans 6:16

The Expositor bible states "Know you not , that to whom you yield yourselves servants to obey, his servant you are to whom you obey so the believer is either a slave to Christ, for that's what the word "servant " means, or else a slave to sin, which he will be if doesn't keep his Faith in Christ and the Cross; whether of sin unto death so once again allow us to state the fact that if the Believer attempts to live for God by any method other than Faith in the finished Work of Christ, the Believer will fail, no matter how hard he or she otherwise tries, or of **obedience unto righteousness?**

The Believer is required to obey the Word of the Lord. He cannot do not that within his own strength, but only by understanding that he receives all things through what Christ did at the Cross and his continued Faith in that finished Work, even on a daily basis. Then the Holy Spirit, Who alone can make us what we ought to be, can accomplish His work within us and in our lives.

So remember you are made righteous through your obedience to hearing God's word with your h**ear**t **ear** because God speaks to your h**ear**t not your head. God is working on the inner man perfecting us inside out and you must keep doing God's word and believing in the finished work at the Cross in Christ, Jes**us** our Lord. And the way in is through Him because in all righteo**us**ness Christ dwells therein. In Jes**us** we have new life and Christ lives in **US**. For we now know that our body is the temple of the Holy Spirit and we are Believers of Christ.

2 Corinthians 10:1-9

Now I Paul myself beseech you by the meekness and gentleness of Christ, who in presence am base among you, but being absent am bold toward you: 2 But I beseech you, that I may not be bold when I am present with that confidence, wherewith I think to be bold against some which think of us as if we walked according to the flesh. 3 For though we walk in the flesh, we do not war after the flesh: 4 For the weapons of our warfare are not carnal, but mighty through God to the pulling down of strong holds; 5 Casting down imaginations, and every high thing that exalteth itself against the knowledge of God, and bringing into captivity every thought to the obedience of Christ. 6 And having in a readiness to revenge all disobedience, when your obedience I fulfilled. 7 Do ye look on things after the outward appearance? If any man trust to himself that he is Christ's let him of himself think this again, that as he is Christ's even so are we Christ's. 8 For though I should boast somewhat more of our authority, edification, and not for your destruction, I should not be ashamed: 9That I may not seem as if I would terrify you by letters.

2 Corinthians 12:1-3

It is not expedient for me doubtless to glory. I will come to visions and revelations of the Lord. 2 I knew a man I Christ above fourteen years ago, (whether in the body, I cannot tell; or whether out of the body, I cannot tell: but God knoweth ;) such an one caught up to the **third heaven**. 3 And I knew such a man, (whether in the body, or out of the body, I cannot tell God knoweth ;)

God has the only way in and we want to get to the third heaven one day to be with the LORD. We know now that God knoweth who is in the body of Christ and not in the body. So enter in the way of Christ and get your heart right for life in Christ.

We must know the way in because wisdom is calling out to us all **Proverbs 8: 1-8**

Says "1. Does not wisdom call out? Dose not understanding raise her voice? 2 On the heights along the way, where the paths meet, she takes her stand; 3 beside the gates leading into the city, at the entrances, she cries aloud: 4 "To you, O men, I call out; I raise my voice to all mankind. 5 You who are simple, gain prudence; you who are foolish, gain understanding. 6 Listen, for I have worthy things to say; I open my lips to speak what is right. 7 My mouth speaks what is true, for my lips detest wickedness. 8 All the words of my mouth are just; none of them is crooked or perverse. Remember wisdom and prudence dwell together prudence is the ability to govern and discipline oneself by the use of reason. The reason is we know that a rational ground or motive will be used as a good reason to act now by God's principle and God's law which leads us on right pathway of the Lord.

(Write notes)

_____

_____

_____

_____

See God in the way of Jesus Christ our Lord and be forgiven all you need to do is ask and believe in Him. Remember this powerful truth: that God is the way and He is the only way, it is Gods way or no way at all. Seek Him and trust Him and live life to the fullest. Amen...

Thank you; please use the correct Kingdom Keys...

Join the **Christian Golf Association** and travel with other Christian Golfers all around the world enjoying life playing golf with other Christian Golfers. We are fellowshipping in Jesus name, please go to the website and join the golf association today and enjoy Life in Christ and play golf with believers and share your faith.

1. Go to www.authorhouse.com or www.golfshot.sampasite.com

2. Click on the book store and enter the book name in the search block.

3. Book name: **A COLLECTION OF SPIRITUAL WORKS**

Thank you for your faithful service to the Kingdom of God and to the people of God, all to the glory of God, in Jes us name.

FAITH WALK

BAGRAM, AIR BASE, AFGHANISTAN 2006-2007

JUST KEEP HOPE ALIVE

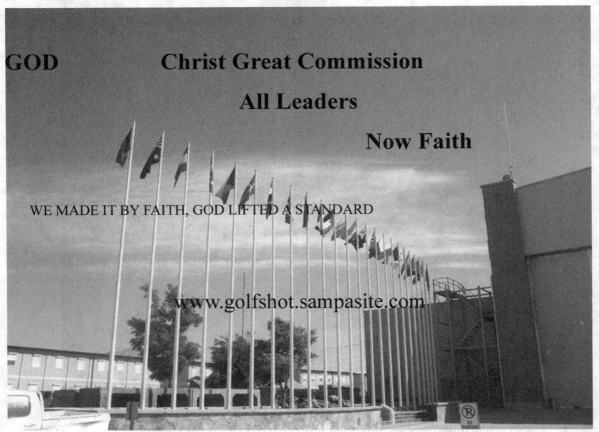

GOD   **Christ Great Commission**

All Leaders

Now Faith

WE MADE IT BY FAITH, GOD LIFTED A STANDARD

www.golfshot.sampasite.com

NO WEAPON FORMED, AGAINST US, SHALL PROSPER

I Need You

I NEED YOU, YOU NEED ME WE'RE ALL APART OF GOD'S BODY STAND WITH ME, AGREE WITH ME WE'RE ALL APART OF GOD'S BODY IT IS HIS WILL THAT EVERYNEED BE SUPPLIED... YOU ARE IMPORTANT TO ME I NEED YOU TO SURVIVE.YOU ARE IMPORTANT TO ME. I NEED YOU TO SURVIVE.

I PRAY FOR YOU, YOU PRAY FOR ME I LOVE YOU, I NEED YOU TO SURVIVE I WON'T HARM YOU WITH WORDS FROM MY MOUTH. I LOVE YOU I NEED YOU TO SURVIVE IT IS HIS WILL THAT EVERY NEED BE SUPPLIED. YOU ARE IMPORTANT TO ME. I NEED YOU TO SURVIVE- Hezekiah Walker

FAITH, LOVE, HOPE, PEACE, IN GOD WE TRUST!!!

Go to the website for ebook: www.csnbooks.com **click on online store look under the ebook section.**
Written by: Evangelist Anthony L. Griffin, while in Afghanistan, Bagram Airbase